Winning
at
Work
A BOOK FOR WOMEN

Dr. Florence Seaman's
Proven Method of Mastering
Crisis Thinking, Guilt, Rejection,
Success, Anger, Criticism, Power, and more

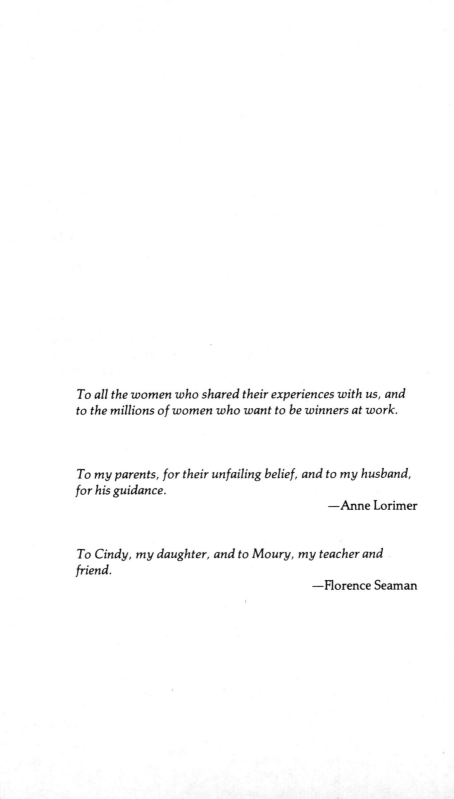

To all the women who shared their experiences with us, and to the millions of women who want to be winners at work.

To my parents, for their unfailing belief, and to my husband, for his guidance.

—Anne Lorimer

To Cindy, my daughter, and to Moury, my teacher and friend.

—Florence Seaman

Winning at Work

A BOOK FOR WOMEN

Dr. Florence Seaman's Proven Method
of Mastering Crisis Thinking, Guilt,
Rejection, Success, Anger,
Criticism, Power, and more.

by Dr. Florence Seaman and Anne Lorimer

RUNNING PRESS
PHILADELPHIA, PENNSYLVANIA

Canadian representatives: John Wiley & Sons Canada Ltd.
22 Worcester Road, Rexdale, Ontario M9W 1L1

International representatives: Kaiman & Polon, Inc.
2175 Lemoine Avenue, Fort Lee, New Jersey 07024

9   8   7   6   5   4   3   2   1
Digit on the right indicates the number of this printing.

LIBRARY OF CONGRESS CATALOGING IN PUBLICATION DATA
Seaman, Florence, 1928–
Winning at work.
Bibliography, p.181
Includes index.
1. Women—Employment—Psychological Aspects.
2. Success.   I. Lorimer, Anne, 1934–   II. Title
HD6053.S268   650'.1'024042   79-19778
ISBN 0-89471-080-X library binding
ISBN 0-89471-079-6 paperback
ISBN 0-89471-093-1 cloth

Cover art direction by James Wizard Wilson
Cover photography by Carl Waltzer
Interior design by Peter John Dorman
Editing by Alida Becker

Typography: Paladium
Typesetting by Linda Gallo, CompArt, Inc., Philadelphia, Pa.
Printed and bound by Port City Press, Baltimore, Md.

This book may be ordered directly from the publisher.
Please include 50 cents postage.

Try your bookstore first.

Running Press
38 South Nineteenth Street
Philadelphia, Pennsylvania 19103

Contents

ACKNOWLEDGMENTS

We wish to thank Dr. Ann Beuf, Coordinator of Womens' Studies at the University of Pennsylvania, for her assistance with several sections of *Winning at Work;* Dr. Morris Aderman of the Illinois Institute of Technology, for his professional advice and concern; and the members of Florence's staff: Jim Dieckman, Jeannette Turner, Ruth Morgan, and Helen Perkinson. Florence would like to express her gratitude to Judy Iammuri and Carolee Risk for their support and insight, and Anne to her first boss, Clare Lilley, Womens' Editor of the *West Chester Daily Local News,* for introducing her to the field. We are also indebted to the hundreds of women who substantiated our clinical data with their personal experiences, particularly the three professional women who shared their stories in the Prologue and Epilogue. Finally, we'd like to thank Sue Golden and Melissa Steingold, who typed the manuscript, and our editor, Alida Becker, for her tireless efforts on our behalf.

Winning
at
Work
A BOOK FOR WOMEN

Dr. Florence Seaman's
Proven Method of Mastering
Crisis Thinking, Guilt, Rejection,
Success, Anger, Criticism, Power, and more

Learning To Be a Winner

Mary and Pamela are both heading for the top. Each woman earns between thirty and forty thousand dollars a year in a job that only a few years ago would have been filled by a man. Neither was born with or married money or power, yet today each wields power in her company and earns a top salary. Mary is the only female personnel director in a large Midwestern company, and Pamela is manager of human resources and development for a corporation in the Southwest. Pamela is also the highest paid black woman on the payroll.

Although there are similarities in their professional experience, their beginnings were quite different. Mary entered the labor force at age thirty following a painful divorce. Until that time she had been a contented homemaker with three small children. She had a high school diploma, but had never planned to go to work. In contrast, Pamela has been plotting her career since the day she entered college.

Neither Mary nor Pamela believe that their success is a fluke, or that other women can't do what they've done. They know that no matter what a woman's goals might be—whether she's working in an office or on an assembly line, or at home with the children—there are basic problems she must solve and patterns she must break in order to achieve the satisfaction, self-respect, and recognition that come with a job well done. Mary and Pamela have learned how to win at work by learning to understand themselves, both as individuals and as women. Listen to how *they* did it, and then we'll show you how *you* can do it too.

————————•———————

MARY: *I was the youngest daughter of an Irish immigrant family: My father only had a sixth grade education, but he worked hard and built up a successful tailoring business. We were raised in a strict but loving home by parents who believed in very different roles for men and women. I was Daddy's girl and knew that I was his favorite, but I never thought that I would go to work like he did. I was raised in the traditional manner to marry, have children, and be supportive of my husband. It never even entered my mind that the day would come when I would be divorced and be the family breadwinner.*

But that day came after twelve years of marriage. My husband was the owner of a small, independent business; I kept his records, entertained his friends and clients, and thoroughly enjoyed my life as a suburban homemaker—until my husband announced that he was leaving me for another woman. The financial settlement agreed on at the time of our divorce wasn't enough for the family's needs, so I was thrust into the job market. Going to work was a nightmare. I was bitter and angry over the divorce and didn't think it was fair that I should have to work when the children were just six, seven, and eight. I was caught between guilt over abandoning my kids and the need for money.

I found a secretarial job in a small company that was a division of a major corporation. During my first weeks on the job, I suffered from a constant backache. The doctor told me that there was nothing organically the matter; the problem was caused by nervous tension. That job was the first time I had ever sat still for eight hours at a time. My desk chair was my

12

prison. I don't think that I'd stayed in one place for more than an hour since my children had been born.

Although career advancement didn't concern me at the time, it certainly was there to be had. All I thought about then was making it through the day, but looking back I know that starting as a secretary in the company was the best move I ever made. A smart secretary can learn how the company works from top to bottom. Today women don't see the tremendous growth potential in this kind of a position. They only look at the gross pay, and not at the benefits offered or the opportunities to move up through the ranks.

I traveled that route myself. I worked hard in my job and soon was given a raise and a better job in the employee relations department. I believe that dedication is all that's needed for advancement within your company. Many women make the mistake of doing a second-rate job because they think that secretarial work is beneath them. As a result, they get a poor performance appraisal, which automatically limits their growth.

Looking back, I think I was given responsibility too quickly—more quickly than I was ready for—but the company was growing, and I grew right along with it. I learned everything I know today in that company, but it wasn't always easy. I took home stacks of work at night, and for the first year or so I really dedicated myself to the job. I'd failed in my marriage, and I didn't want to fail in my job too. I was frightened that I would make a mistake—but when I did, I often got more upset than my boss did. As I got more comfortable, I stopped believing that I had to be perfect. My self-confidence had been shattered by the divorce, and at the beginning I honestly didn't believe that I was as good as the next person. I worked much harder because I thought that anybody could do my job better and quicker.

I know that my lack of a college education contributed to my

13

sense of inadequacy. I was advanced to the job of personnel relations consultant when the former consultant left. It was the top personnel job in the company, and I served on the job evaluation committee with four men. At first I felt uptight about my lack of a formal education and wondered what I was doing there with four PhDs. Then I realized that I understood employee problems and job overlaps better than they did because I had worked my way up in the company; I knew everybody and heard everything. I was an important resource. I think that may have been the turning point in my career because from then on I began to realize that I had developed specific and valuable abilities.

No sooner was I comfortable in my new job than I was approached to interview for the job of personnel director with the parent company. The thought of leaving was a wrench for me because I trusted my company and knew everybody. Although there was no more growth potential in my job, it was becoming more time-consuming because the company was growing at a fantastic rate. When I was first divorced, that job had been my whole life, but I had developed other outside activities. The new position offered me an irresistible combination of more money and more free time.

I don't consider myself aggressive or career oriented, and I haven't plotted any long-term goals. I've never had a mentor, but there have always been people in the company who seem to look out for me and let me know when a good job is about to be available. I don't plan ahead, but good things keep happening. I've always listened when a friend suggested that I interview for a different position.

Now I do the interviewing. I handle the hiring of a hundred secretarial and administrative employees each month, and that's given me a lot of insight into how women approach their work. It seems to me that some women come on too strong. I'm *most apt to hire an enthusiastic, cheerful woman who knows a bit about the company and why she'd like to work for us. For example, we offer our employees a great many free educational programs. If a woman plans to enroll in college for her BA at the company's expense, she's making the same kind of commitment to us that we're making to her.*

I've also noticed that women aren't as trusting of other women as they are of men. They don't believe me when I tell them that the company perks and benefits offset a lower salary. Many women also dislike taking risks—but my profession, personnel, is a risk-taking one. Every time I hire an employee, I'm taking a risk. I learn from my mistakes—and I've made some—and I try to live with them. I know that if I make too many, I'm going to be out of a job, but I try to be honest about my errors instead of hiding them. I don't respect people who blame their mistakes on a secretary or a typist instead of taking the responsibility themselves.

I've noticed too that women have a greater tendency to make scenes than men. Often they'll reprimand a subordinate in front of other people so that they'll look bigger themselves. Women teach manners to their children, but they don't always practice them themselves. A company needs employees who can get along with each other.

Women also tend to be far more guarded about themselves than men, particularly the ones who are returning to work after a long absence. I wish I were still allowed to ask them about their families, because a woman relaxes when she talks about her kids—just like men relax over sports. It used to be a good way to break the ice in an interview. It may sound like heresy, but equal opportunity laws have sometimes dehumanized the woman-to-woman relationship.

As a woman, I have to admit that emotion sometimes gets in my way. I remember one time when I was afraid I might burst into tears. I was pushing for an employee who deserved a pro-

motion. She had some rough edges and came on a bit on the tough side, but I knew she was right for the job. The hiring decision was up to the four other directors and me. I was fine in the meeting until the men began to get louder and louder. One in particular wanted to shout me down, and accused me of not listening to him simply because I didn't agree with him. I was afraid I might burst into tears, but luckily I'd taken the time before the meeting to write down all the facts of the situation and my reasons for wanting to hire the girl. When I felt myself becoming emotional, I was able to get back under control by concentrating on my facts.

I don't plan to stay in my present job indefinitely, but I haven't decided on my next step. When the time is right, something new will present itself, as long as I do my best in this job. After all, I've gone a long way—from secretary to executive— in just ten years, so I have every reason to feel confident about what I'm doing now, and what I may be doing ten years from now.

PAMELA: *When I was ten years old I wanted to go to a summer camp, so I went out and got every kind of job a ten-year-old could do until I made enough money. My parents taught us that we wouldn't know how much we could do until we tried. They respected our individuality, supported us in whatever we chose, and never pitted us against each other. I think my self-confidence goes back to those early lessons. We were a very middle-class family. My father worked two jobs, and when we were old enough to go to school my mother did clerical work. My parents believed in education, but they refused to let us take out any college loans. They wanted each of their three children to embark on adult life educated and unencumbered.*
I was very close to my father when I was growing up. My father could watch the world fall apart and then logically and

systematically put it back together piece by piece. My com-
posure under pressure comes from him; we're both stubborn.
When I was a kid I used to start off using a logical argument for
something I wanted to do. If that didn't work, I burst into tears.
I had the best of both worlds and usually got my way. I have to
admit that I'm still getting my way. I'm mildly aggressive, go
after what I want, and learn what I need to know. I have a good
feeling about myself and my capabilities—I know that I'll suc-
ceed in whatever I try.

I graduated from a local college with a degree in English and
was headed for a teaching career, but I was frustrated by the
roadblocks I saw in the system. I knew that I couldn't go to
school each day with a rotten attitude, so I decided to get the
MA I'd need to teach at the college level. To make the money
for my tuition, I took a job with a major electronics company
as a very, very assistant market researcher. I've been with the
company ever since.

I lucked out with my first job. My supervisor was an astute
market analyst who trained me well. I stayed in the department
for five years and was running it when I left. I think my success
in the company is partially the result of planning a career path
for myself, meeting my goals, and moving on—and up. My
next job was in another branch of the company, where I learned
the ropes of market analysis and sales forecasting—and a lot
about the company at the same time. After two and a half
years, I decided that I didn't want to spend my life as an
analyst. I knew what I liked about my job and made two
decisions—I wanted to stay with the company, but in an area
that gave me more growth potential. Since I like people and
survey work, personnel and public affairs seemed to fit the bill.

I believe in being direct. I told my boss that I wanted to move
and asked him to help me find another job in the company. At
first he tried to persuade me to stay, but when he saw that I was

determined to move he directed me to a position as a consultant in the department of human resources and development, which plans training sessions, teaches courses for employees, and provides employee counseling. I worked as a consultant for two years until the training director of the department left and I moved up. Now I'm the manager of the department. I handle all employee communications and enjoy organizing the company's teaching programs. I've come full circle, back to where I started—teaching. But I don't intend to stay where I am. In three years I plan to be the director of personnel for the whole metropolitan area.

My stubbornness—others might call it determination—has helped me to reach the top. If I think a program will work I just won't take no for an answer. When I worked for the vice president in market research I believed that our sales representatives weren't receiving adequate training. My boss considered training an expense, but I saw it as an investment. I was stubborn and kept asking for a chance to try out my ideas. I knew that if I got the go-ahead there was no way that I wasn't going to make it work. Finally, my boss gave in and let me have an extra day at one of our regional sales conferences. It was so successful that extra training days have become part of company policy at sales conferences all across the country. And now I'm planning an additional series of manager training seminars.

I take risks all the time. My first training day for the regional sales conference was a big risk and would have been an expensive one if the company hadn't benefited. But I won't take a foolish risk. At the same time, I know that my ability to stick my neck out has gotten me where I am today.

During my years in sales and research, I knew everything that went on in the company—and usually I knew it before my boss. You don't succeed in a company by sitting in your office waiting for people to tell you things. When I became a consul-

tant in the human resources department, I was given a client group to help. At first nobody brought their problems to me, but I kept myself highly visible and familiar. I strolled around the office, said 'hello,' and let people know I was there. Pretty soon they began coming in with their difficulties. I help people solve problems by identifying all the available alternatives, but then I let them make the decisions themselves. I let people keep the ownership of their problems; I won't rescue them.

It isn't easy to be the highest paid black woman in the corporation. I don't have peers and I've always refused to be the token black for the blacks or the token woman for the women. I'm also aware that most of my jobs have been the kind that used to be reserved for men. Since many of my dealings are with men, I've had to learn the male business rules. At regional sales conferences there are usually about twenty-five men—and me. I see myself as an equal and active participant in the conference room, not as a woman. I never question my right to be there, and I raise my voice right along with the men. On the other hand, I'm not about to deny my femininity. Although I travel with men, I am still a woman. I like having doors opened for me and my chair held. It's fine with me if somebody else wants to pick up the check.

Success has its rewards, but it can be lonely at the top. I feel that I'm on stage most of the time and must continually prove myself. Loneliness is the price of success. You tend to lose the friends you made when you started with the company. I'm now at a level where I'm privy to a lot of confidential information, and this sets me apart from my old friends. I don't have anything in common with the people I used to buddy around with.

My husband is my best friend. He's the director of labor relations for a supermarket chain. We don't have any children.

We're both independent people, but we do a lot together. For a while I made more money than he did, but my husband didn't object; he has a healthy ego. He knew that I made more money because I was in a better company, not because I was better than he was. And from the very beginning we've agreed that whoever got the best business opportunity would take it, and the other would follow.

I'm on the road twenty-five percent of the time because of my training seminars and liaison programs with universities. Frankly I get tired of being asked what my husband thinks of my traveling. You know, I never asked him about it—travel is simply one requirement of my job. When I travel, I visit friends in different cities; I've made a lot of them through the company. If I don't have a social engagement I read, prepare my work for the next day, and watch television. I don't go to the bar for the evening.

Recently my husband came along to a sales convention that included programs for wives. He had a marvelous time as the only male spouse, attending cooking classes and going on trips with "his girls." Now he can make a great steak Diane.

Home for us is a house in the suburbs with a housekeeper to keep it running smoothly. My job is high powered and very demanding, so sometimes I have to stop and take care of myself for a while. I garden, plant a bush, play raquetball, or soak in a tub full of bubbles while I read a book. I sing in my church choir, but I miss not having the time to take an active role in other community affairs. I travel too much to make that possible.

The only thing in this world that I really fear is getting pregnant. Ten years ago I would have made the sacrifice and given up my career for a family because I believe that a mother belongs at home with her children. But today I'm a hundred-

percent career woman who likes her lifestyle. I don't feel that I'm avoiding my duty to God or my country by not having kids.

My parents taught me to go ahead and try for anything I wanted, and I like where I've gotten by trying. I plan to make as much money as I can and do whatever I want to do. If a better offer comes from a different company I'll take it. I want to keep moving up.

CHAPTER 1

Goodbye Guilt

————————◦•▸◦——————————

As a child you feel guilty when you sneak a cookie, as a teenager you feel guilty when you lie to your mother, and as an adult you feel guilty when you choose a career over full-time homemaking. Guilt is the conflict between being taught to do one thing and actually doing another, the difference between saying "I have to" or "I should" and "I want to"—and then doing the latter. It's that uncomfortable feeling you get when you violate a legal, moral, ethical, social, or psychological principle. Guilt hangs us up, holds us back, and hampers our performance.

Let's face it. Guilt can be a crippling emotion. When you feel guilty you punish and blame yourself and remain in a constant state of misery which limits your potential. Your guilt comes from having a conscience, a little inner voice that tells you what's right and wrong. To rid yourself of guilt you need to evaluate that voice in terms of what *you*—not your parents or society—believe is right.

Our society still teaches that little girls are less important than little boys and that when they're grown up they can't attain the same goals. Although these views are changing, many people still believe that personal fulfillment outside the home should only apply to men.

Goodbye Guilt

As recently as five years ago, Dr. Ann Beuf's survey of kindergarten children uncovered some interesting facts about the way they saw themselves. One little girl said that if she were a boy she would fly like a bird—anything as grand as flight was not possible for a girl. She said she'd like to be a pilot or a doctor, but added that she'd probably be a nurse or a stewardess. When a little boy was asked what he would be if he were a girl he simply covered his face with his hands and put his head down on the desk. The prospect was too terrible to contemplate. Finally, he mumbled, "If I were a girl I guess I'd just have to grow up to be nothing."

Guilt didn't come in your genes. According to cultural anthropologist Abraham Kardener, guilt is learned. It occurs in a culture that has specific child-rearing patterns such as parental punishment for disobedience and love for obedience. If your mother hugs you for playing with your baby sister but spanks you for tripping her, you quickly learn to feel guilty for doing what you feel like.

Your guilt feeling can be traced back to your parents' value system and to the political, socioeconomic, and sexual habits you were exposed to as a child. Most of the values you live by don't reflect your own input, but you've lived by them and made them a habit because you've been brought up with them. It's likely that when you take the time to analyze them you won't choose to keep all of them.

A value system is an arbitrary set of rules of right and wrong by which people judge the behavior of others. Value systems are established by society and passed along through customs and traditions, many of which may become more and more archaic. Parents, teachers, and religious leaders all had a part in building your value system. They taught you about honesty, the value of work, morality, and respect. Some of the values passed on to you are tried and true for all generations, but others are not the absolutes our parents tell us. They tend to be relative to the time we're born. For example, if you're forty or fifty, you were probably taught to handle conflict by turning the other cheek. Today's teenager is more assertive and more apt to stand up for her rights. When you were a teenager, you didn't think you *had* any rights.

Today's working woman must cope with any number of conflicts in her value system. The seventies mark a decade of social change. Equal rights amendments in many states guarantee women equality with men on the job. More women are working than ever before in the nation's history, including half of all the mothers of school-age children. Yet many of these forty million working women complain of feeling guilty and uncomfortable on the job. They've been brought up to be wives and mothers who stay at home and nurture their families. They feel guilty when they seek a career outside of the home because of the conflict between what they want to do and what they feel they ought to be doing. Their value systems haven't caught up with their options, and although they can do things their mothers never dreamed of, they're not happy doing them.

A large number of working women who attend Florence's guilt workshops complain of feeling uncomfortable and vaguely uneasy at work—"as if something is going to happen." They believe that this feeling must somehow be related to their job, and are frustrated when they can't isolate a specific cause. The difficulty is that their conflict is rooted in their value system, not in their job. They've followed the call of the women's movement, shifted gears, gone to work, and made all the external changes—but they haven't coped with the persistent inner voice that tells them they ought to be home taking care of the kids. Intellectually, they believe in the emerging new femininity that sanctions mother's role at the office—but deep inside they remain trapped in the cultural stereotype that tells them to cook, clean, and be home when the kids get off the school bus. They feel guilty.

Labor Department figures show that as of March 1978, there were 11.1 million married couples with children under six. In almost 42 percent of those families, the wife was either holding a job or looking for work—as compared to only 30 percent in 1970 and 19 percent in 1960.

When there are young children at home it's hard for mothers not to feel guilty. But according to Ralph Smith, author of *The Subtle Revolution: Women at Work*, it isn't at all clear that the number of hours spent with a parent are critical to a child's development. As Smith reminds us, "Contrary to the imaginings of many guilt-ridden working mothers, full-time homemakers do not spend most of their days in stimulating or affectionate play with their children."

Such facts are corroborated by women like Edna, a college professor who discovered that she spends more time with her children now than she did when she was a full-time mother. "Since the kids and I were together all the time I got terribly bored and spent a lot of my time talking to friends on the telephone or going to another mother's house to talk to her while the children amused themselves. Now that my schedule is full, I find that I'm arranging quality time and projects for the children. We're all enjoying each other more."

It's interesting to note that guilt is caused by the reason *why* you're working, not the *fact* of working. Women have worked side by side with their husbands since the very beginnings of our country. And there are millions of women who get up every day and go to work in boring, unchallenging jobs and are not bothered by the tiniest twinge of guilt. Their paychecks go for a child's college education, the mortgage, or new drapes. They don't feel guilty about working because they're working for their family's fulfillment, not their own. Guilt comes from going to work because you *want* to, not because you *have* to. You're afraid that your job may take something away from your family or a relationship rather than enhance it. The emotionally healthy woman is able to integrate achievement and mothering with other aspects of her life and to enjoy all of them.

Caroline was totally bewildered by her guilt over a new job when she attended Florence's workshop. She had worked for years as a telephone solicitor, part-time saleswoman, and teacher's aid to help with the family finances—and she'd never felt guilty. Spurred on by the women's movement and a consciousness-raising group, she decided that she wanted to become a real estate saleswoman. She passed her exams and got a job, which she almost quit. "I felt terribly uncomfortable being away from the family when I thought I ought to be home baking cookies. The peculiar thing was that I hadn't been home before and it had never bothered me—but because I loved the business I felt as if I were choosing it and not my family. If my husband hadn't been supportive I know that I would have quit."

Similar guilt feelings kept Pat, another workshop participant, from following through with a career. Pat had dropped out of college to marry. She had devoted her energy to being Supermom and Superwife, trying to convince herself that she was happy in spite of regular bouts of depression. She baked every cake the *Ladies' Home Journal* suggested and entertained her children's friends and her husband's business associates, but her depression wasn't cured until she decided to return to college. Her family supported her decision because she didn't let her education interfere with their lives. She dovetailed her classes with her children's schedules and never felt guilty—just constantly fatigued from juggling the roles of wife, mother, and student. Like many women, she felt compulsive about continuing to do everything she had done before.

Goodbye Guilt

Guilt sabotaged her when she graduated. "I was offered a management position that included some travel. I was thrilled, but then felt so guilty about wanting to take the job and be away from home that I turned it down. It went against my idea of what a wife and mother should be. I had opportunities for other jobs, but whenever I figured out the time they'd take from my family I felt panicky. In the end, I decided to go on with my education because that was an acceptable way of getting out of the house and didn't put me into a conflict." Pat's case shows that *thoughts* can make us feel just as guilty as actions can. Wanting to travel was all it took to make her feel guilty.

Often guilt doesn't surface until a woman switches to the big time from a small, cottage industry (such as making Christmas candles, dried flower arrangements, or appliqued aprons). Jill, the mother of three teenagers, started a small tennis camp for girls. The camp was a family affair because all of her children taught there in the summer. Her philosophy of cultivating confidence through tennis and tennis through confidence caught hold and soon she was operating her camp in four different locations with four directors. Then she received requests to open branches in different states, and along with her success came conflict. Did she want to become a full-time businesswoman or did she want to keep some of her time free to travel with her husband and be with her children? For the moment, Jill has decided to keep her business small because being a wife and mother are more important roles for her.

Working women with children may have the most obvious conflicts with the traditional female role, but they aren't the only ones who are plagued by guilt. Childless women in two-career families are troubled by issues that can range from the vital question of who quits their job when the other gets an offer in another city to the seemingly petty question of who stays home from work to let in a repairman. In most families, with or without children, it's the woman whose job comes second. She feels resentful when she has to defer to the needs of her husband's job, and then she feels guilty because her early training has emphasized a women's duty to be supportive to her husband. After all, he's the breadwinner and she's the helpmate— or so she was taught.

It's common for men and women to share the housekeeping chores in two-job families, but if the wife gives up her job, she automatically shoulders all the wash, shopping, and cleaning. She would feel guilty if she didn't. "I loved working, but I hated all the responsibilities that are expected of a homemaker," said Louise, a publisher's assistant who finally returned to work to escape the "prison" of the house.

When Susan and her husband married, they agreed to a housework contract. But when Susan lost her job, she felt that it was only fair for her to take over all the chores. "I despised it. I'd rather break dishes than wash them. I need to work to feel worthy, and I don't find anything worthwhile in housework. On the other hand, I feel guilty if I don't do it." Needless to say, Susan is also back at work.

Even single women are not immune to guilt. Some women who choose a career over marriage and children discover when they reach their mid-thirties that they feel guilty about having made that decision. A thirty-five-year-old editor of children's books puts it this way, "When I was twenty, I felt guilty about not marrying because my mother had convinced me that every woman needed a husband, but I made a determined effort to put my career first. Now I'm discovering that I'm a casualty of the women's movement. My child-bearing years are almost over, and I wonder if I've missed something. I feel guilty about my decision."

One college PhD expressed it this way, "Suddenly I look at all the degrees on my wall and wonder if it was worth it. Did I make the right decision? Would I rather be weeding the garden and thinking about my first grandchild? As I get older, the family that I didn't have becomes more important, and I have a greater need to belong to the next generation."

Wondering about what might have been is part of human nature, but that backward glance doesn't have to mean that you made a mistake. Carol is a top public relations director, respected and sought after in her field. She made a conscious decision not to have children when she married ten years ago and has never regretted it. "I knew from the beginning that I wasn't the maternal type, and I never felt that a baby would establish my womanhood. In fact, to have a baby for that reason would have been very selfish. But I do have a side of me that needs to nurture. When you don't satisfy that kind of impulse it can get you into trouble; you'll run around trying to help people who don't need it or won't benefit from it. I meet my nurturing needs through a close relationship with my retarded nephew. It helps me and him *and* his mother, who has six other children."

In contrast to the childless woman, the married woman who decides to pursue a career in her thirties or forties frequently faces a guilt conflict over leaving the nest along with the children. She, who has been home with the kids for fifteen or twenty years of her life, is ready to try her wings. On the other hand, her husband, who has been aggressively fighting in the business arena, may be getting ready to come home to the nest, putter about the backyard, and watch TV.

The forty-year-old man often yearns for home and hearth; his middle years are a time when he's reappraising his life and accepting compromises he may not have considered in his youth. His hair is receding, his paunch is increasing, and he knows that he may not ever reach the top of his company. But his wife is confronted by the issue of self-declaration. When she was thirty she may have felt that she would drown without a man, but at forty she may want to prove that she can make it on her own. And yet she may also have a nagging feeling of guilt that she doesn't have the right to feel so eager to conquer the world when her husband seems to have decided to call a ceasefire. The forties are a common age for women to remarry or run away; they're also a time for women to enter or reenter the working world—and many of them feel guilty about doing it.

Cindy, a bright, well-dressed real estate saleswoman, discussed this conflict at one of Florence's workshops. "I'd been at home with kids for eighteen years while my husband travelled the globe and worked late at night. When the kids were all in senior high school I decided to go to work because so many of my friends seemed trapped in a life of country club tennis, too many cocktails, or too many tranquilizers. I thought my husband would be pleased and supportive. Instead, he was really threatened. Suddenly he was planning weekend work projects and even started building a greenhouse for me, while I went buzzing off to work—the weekend is my big selling time. Naturally I felt guilty about abandoning him, particularly after all the years I'd begged him to stay home with the family on the weekends. Don't think that he didn't remind me of that either. Well, eventually we worked the problem through and made a few compromises, but it's taken time. My extra income allows me to travel with him for the first time in our marriage, so we substitute business trips for weekends. He had always wanted a boat, so we bought a secondhand one that he works on every weekend. Once a month I take off from work and we spend the weekend sailing together. But the best part is that now I hear by the grapevine that he boasts about my success to his friends."

Cindy and her husband have resolved their mid-life crisis and improved their relationship so that both of them are able to feel joy in their accomplishments. Men and women who haven't resolved these kinds of differences complain of feeling bored, stale, and blue—as if they have nothing to live for. Couples can survive this transitional period with their marriages intact only if they take the time to talk about their feelings and their needs—and understand the sources of their guilt and resentment.

It helps for a woman to remember her husband's early training. A man who has been brought up to protect and care for women is often baffled by a woman's angry "I can do it myself" when he opens the door, holds the chair, or lights her cigarette. Most likely he grew up with a full-time mother at home and has translated this model to his wife.

Keep all this in mind, and you won't be surprised if your husband is threatened by your desire for a job. Since you're going to be taking something away from his role as a provider, try to strike a new balance by giving something back. Your paycheck will lift the burden from his shoulders so he won't have to be the sole support of the family. Some men who've been stuck in boring jobs for years have discovered that a working wife allows them more options for change.

Help your husband to adjust by letting him know that you'll continue to need him emotionally, even though you aren't as financially dependent as you once were. Your sensitivity to both his needs and his value system is going to make the transitional period easier for both of you. And you might find, like Nancy and her husband did, that there are unexpected bonuses in store. "I felt very guilty about my husband and our relationship when I got a job," she admitted. However, Nancy discovered that once the family got used to it, her job added a new dimension to her marriage. "We had more to talk about than the kids and in many ways we spent more quality time together. We even arranged to meet for dinner downtown several nights a week."

———•———

Women who are caught in the guilt trap sometimes punish themselves by not achieving their working potential. According to Alexis Herman, director of the Womens' Bureau of the Department of Labor, an agency which promotes and advances the welfare of working women, most of the forty million women working today are holding the same kinds of jobs women held thirty years ago. They are the nation's clerks, typists, secretaries, teachers, saleswomen, and waitresses. Seventy-five percent of all working women remain trapped in low-paying clerical, service, or factory occupations. Two thirds of the nation's professional women are either teachers or nurses.

Although women have made inroads into the corporate world at a middle-management level, many of the new female executives are actually low-level personnel with fancy titles. Many companies may seem to comply with the new affirmative action programs, but only a small minority of their female employees are really involved in corporate decision-making.

Although many of the reasons for this situation are certainly not the fault of women, it *is* true that guilty women punish themselves by not living up to their potential. Because they don't feel that they deserve the rewards of success, they start projects and never finish them or build barriers to prevent themselves from accomplishing their goals.

Sarah was given the job of preparing a manual that would outline all the aspects of her company's affirmative action program. She was well qualified for the job, and her successful handling of the project would probably have resulted in a promotion. Despite her boss's encouragement, Sarah was unable to complete the job. She was never satisfied, and kept rewriting and rewriting until another person was assigned to help her. Eventually the project was finished, but Sarah was passed over for a promotion.

Goodbye Guilt

Some women feel unworthy because they're afraid they won't do well enough, that they'll let down the people who have helped them. The housewife who returns to college fears that she will let her family down by flunking out, the mother who has enlisted her family's help with the housekeeping fears that she will be fired.

This kind of guilt comes from believing that you must live up to someone else's expectations, that receiving help somehow compromises your achievements. Instead of feeling unworthy of help, remember that the most rewarding relationships are two-way ones. When you help your child with his homework, you're responding to his need because you care about him, not because you expect him to get a perfect mark.

You can get out of this kind of guilt trap by telling your family in advance that you appreciate their help and will do the best you can—but your best is *all* that you can promise. Remind them that you may not succeed, and help them to keep their goals and expectations realistic. You'll have a hard time being a straight-A student if you're going to continue doing all the cooking, cleaning, and chauffeuring.

Caught in a very different guilt trap, some women feel uneasy about choosing to *remain* a homemaker. They have absorbed so many tenets of the liberation movement that they wonder if they *ought* to be working. In some cases, they take on jobs that they don't really want merely to get rid of the stigma of being "just a housewife." In a recent issue of *The Christian Science Monitor*, a young woman defended her choice to be a housewife and mother: "From the time I get up in the morning to cook breakfast for the kids until the minute I sit down after dinner I am working in my chosen profession. My 'business day' has importance to me and to every other life I touch." Feeling guilty about the personal fulfillment you receive from homemaking is just as unhealthy—and unnecessary—as feeling guilty about your pleasure in any other job.

In many cases, the conflict caused by guilt can give you an exaggerated sense of your own power and make you feel responsible for events over which you have no control. If your child falls off his bike while you're at work you automatically assume that it wouldn't have happened if you'd been there. Somehow, the accident is your fault.

During a round-table discussion, several workshop participants admitted that they weren't troubled by any guilt until two-thirty in the afternoon, when the kids got home from school—unless a child was sick, and then they felt guilty all day. One of the women summed up the situation this way, "I wasted the last two hours of the working day worrying about my kids, who were happily sitting in front of the TV with a competent babysitter munching on cookies. They didn't miss me a bit. If I wanted to worry, it would have made better sense to worry about getting mugged or about the car getting stolen."

People who are caught in a guilt trap give themselves away by overjustifying, overexplaining, and overdefending their actions. Such behavior often creates additional problems. When you feel secure in your decisions and are free from guilt, all you need to do is make a simple statement. For example, if you accept working late as a part of your job, you simply call home and tell your husband that you'll be late. If you feel guilty, you pick up the telephone and square off for battle, defending your right to work late or overexplaining the colossal amount of work you have to do. Many husbands are confused by such an approach and may worry that you're covering something up. They don't realize that the person you're actually arguing with is *yourself*.

Women also cope with guilt by atoning for their actions. For example, Jessica divorced her husband and returned to college, much to her parents' dismay. They didn't believe in divorce, or in education for women. Jessica atoned for violating her parents' value system by taking ten years to complete her degree.

—————•—————

When it comes to guilt, you can be your own worst enemy— but you aren't the *only* enemy. Others will often try to hang a guilt trip on you too. People use guilt as a way to avoid their own responsibilities. They'll dump it on anybody who'll accept the blame—and if you haven't worked out your own value system you're likely to be on the receiving end. Women are particularly vulnerable when someone says "you made me do it" because they've been socialized to accept that sort of responsibility. (You'll learn more about this later, in Chapter 8.) It helps to remember that you're not God, that everybody is responsible for their own actions.

Ruth started as a secretary in a major corporation but was promoted to the position of equipment demonstrator. She traveled around the country showing clients how to use office equipment, and she loved every minute of it. She was living with a man whose job also involved travel, but they managed to mesh their schedules. After a year, Ruth's company transferred her division to Washington, and offered her an even better job along with the move. Ruth's companion was threatened by her promotion and declared that if she loved him she would keep the arrangement as it was and remain in their joint home in Boston. Ruth had been brought up to believe that a woman belonged at home, so she followed that early training and gave up her new job. She kept house and resumed her old secretarial job. In the beginning, she didn't resent the sacrifice because she was in love, but as time passed she was left with bitter dreams of what she might have achieved if her companion had not made her feel so guilty.

"If you love me, you'll give up your job." It was a message to which Ruth was very vulnerable. Had she been able to separate herself from her guilt feelings, she would have realized that love is a giving and sharing of two *autonomous* people. They may zig and zag in their priorities, but they never make one partner subservient to the other all the time.

You can avoid taking on other people's guilt if you can concentrate on assuming your own responsibilities at work and at home and accepting the consequences of a particular action. And remember that when you feel guilty you will often only see one solution to a problem—the one that makes you feel the worst. But there is *always* more than one solution.

Once you've given in to guilt it can affect almost every aspect of your life. When you allow yourself to be trapped in the self-destructive cycle of punishment and atonement you become very vulnerable. Not only do you deny yourself the pleasure of relaxation, enjoyment, and peace, but you set yourself up to be manipulated by the people around you. The guilty mother becomes a weekend drudge, and the guilty wife is at her husband's beck and call. But you don't have to be a slave to your guilt. Mount a Guilt Offensive today.

Step one is to reassess your value system and determine its relevance. Make a list of all the values you've been living by and ask yourself if they work for you. Remember that you're old enough to choose your *own* values. You don't have to borrow somebody else's.

Step two is to restructure your value system to suit the person you are. Keep the values that fit, but change those that are no longer consistent with the way you choose to live; your value system belongs *entirely* to you and should reflect your personality. Once you understand the differences between your old value system and your new one, you won't be as vulnerable to other people's guilt trips.

Step three is to make guilt work *for* you not *against* you. Once you have structured your own value system, pay attention to your twinges of guilt. If you feel uncomfortable about a decision, you may need to look at the issue more closely to analyze the source of your discomfort. If the consequences of an action appear to be too great, you may decide that you're better off opting against it.

Step four is to talk about your guilt feelings with the people who are close to you. This will not only lighten your load; you may also discover that your friends and family don't expect you to do all the things you thought they did. When you share your concerns, you're allowing others to actively support your decisions.

While you're charting your guilt offensive, remember one final piece of advice—be patient with yourself. You won't be able to change a lifetime of socialization overnight, but every step you take will set you further along on your way to a guilt-free existence.

CHAPTER 2

Ride Out Rejection

———————————

Rejection is part of everyday life, and yet it's still a painful experience for many women. They take rejection personally, they believe that it is *they* who are being rejected, not simply their idea or their opinion. "Whenever I turn down my assistant's suggestion for a stock purchase she gets uptight," says an exasperated executive in the trust department of a bank. "I'm rejecting the company she wants to invest in, not *her*."

Webster's dictionary defines the verb reject as "to refuse to take, to throw out, or discard as worthless," and most women agree that being rejected certainly makes them feel worthless. When you're rejected, an inner voice often whispers, "See, I told you all along you weren't any good."

The fear of rejection can keep capable women sitting at home or doing telephone solicitation or volunteer work instead of aggressively scouting the job market. An employment counselor who works with these women used the story of Kate to show just how devastating rejection can be. Kate was an intelligent, well-dressed mother of four with years of experience as a volunteer. Many of her skills were valuable in the job market, and the counselor was positive that Kate would land a job after several interviews—and she would have if she had gone to more than one interview.

The average number of interviews for a woman re-entering the job market is three. Men are well aware that they will need to send out a hundred resumes for every four interviews they receive, and that from those four there will probably be only one firm job offer. But Kate, like many women, expected to be hired instantly or never. She was devastated when she was turned down for a job in the public relations department of a rehabilitation hospital. It made no difference that she almost got the job, or that her lack of actual public relations work was the only negative factor involved.

Kate was convinced that she was rejected because she was an inadequate person. Not only did she give up looking for another job, she also built up a complicated set of defenses. She rejected the job market before it could reject her. Kate convinced herself that she had chosen not to work because she could afford not to, that she preferred the emotional rewards of volunteer work, and that she was primarily interested in serving her community. They were all perfectly good motives, but they weren't the truth. Afraid of rejection, Kate was unwilling to take another risk.

Like Kate, you aren't going to get over the rejection hurdle until you look beneath the surface and examine your own defenses and your excuses for giving up. If you have difficulty accepting and dealing with rejection, it's likely that you have an exaggerated need for approval. And that's only natural. After all, women are trained people-pleasers.

Men cope better with rejection because they've been socialized more strongly in their appropriate sex role behavior. Little boys switch their identification from mother to father at an early age and discover that they're punished—rejected—for any "sissy" holdovers like crying or playing with dolls. Lessons like these that are learned early in life are more deeply engrained than those learned at a later time.

Highly masculine males are those whose fathers have been dominant and decisive in setting limits and giving rewards and punishments. But while a father responds to his son as a demanding and critical parent, he is often permissive, warm, and indulgent towards his daughter.

Although a girl's femininity is related to both her father's masculinity and his approval of her mother as a model, Florence's clinical experience has shown that it is a girl's mother who most influences a girl's attitude towards rejection in later life. The girl who is rejected by her mother will be suspicious and fearful of rejection as an adult. She may either avoid friendships with other women or seek them with women who remind her of her mother, hoping that they, unlike her mother, will accept her. She may also adopt a rejecting attitude toward others as a defense against being hurt.

Rejection by our mothers may or may not always be something that we're conscious of. Stephanie's mother treated her very well in public, but was given to fits of irrational temper at home. At times she would beat Stephanie with a wooden spoon until it broke or slam her head against a wall so hard that Stephanie would have a headache for days. Stephanie had always been taught that family members never discussed private matters outside their home, so she never told anybody about her mother's behavior. For a long time, Stephanie believed that all mothers were like hers—and that *she* was unlovable. After she herself had married, she told a neighbor about her mother, and "the look on her face was so shocked that I realized I had grown up very differently than most girls."

Stephanie remains suspicious of other women. She has chosen to teach nursery school because three-year-olds are a nonthreatening, nonrejecting group. She envies women who lunch together and shop together, but is unable to make any overture to join them for fear of being rejected. "I envied my neighbors who got together with their toddlers for morning coffee, just stopping at each other's houses, but I didn't have the confidence to go anywhere unless I was invited. Now I realize that my neighbors thought I was standoffish."

Lisa's mother rejected her in a less direct fashion, but the effects have been just as devastating. Whenever Lisa had an idea, her mother had a better one. She would start by commending Lisa, but then would add, "I wonder if you've considered. . . ." and by the time she was finished Lisa had abandoned her own idea and followed her mother's. To be accepted, she did things her mother's way. "I grew up feeling very insecure about my decision-making capabilities, and although I became more secretive about my ideas, I still lacked self-confidence. When I went to work, I always seemed to set myself up in a mother-daughter relationship with my boss or with a coworker. I felt that I needed to be told what to do, and then I hated the person who told me."

Women who become dependent on others at work tend to let their performance suffer when they feel rejected. Tracy had established a mother-daughter relationship with her boss during the year that she was going through a divorce. She felt threatened when a second woman was added to her department, particularly when her boss appeared to develop an equally close relationship with the new woman. Fear of rejection made Tracy lose sight of the bottom line in the business world— performance on the job. As Tracy's work suffered, the second woman received some of her assignments. Frustrated and fearful, Tracy blamed everybody in the department for her inability to get her work done. Inevitably, she was fired for her lack of performance.

People often respond to rejection with the syndrome that might be called *Now You Too Know I'm No Good.* If you already suffer from feelings of low self-esteem and self-worth, the imagined or real rejection of another person reinforces those negative self-images you've been carrying around since childhood.

Miriam's fear of rejection was severely limiting her potential at work. New company affirmative action programs offered her an opportunity to move out of the personnel department and into a sales position. Although she wanted to expand her horizons, she was afraid to leave her safe slot. Miriam was bright and had good intuition. It was obvious not only to her supervisor but to everyone who met her that she was a natural for the sales job. But Miriam was so afraid of being rejected by the other members of the sales group that she was unwilling to give the new position a try.

The reasons for Miriam's unreasonable fear of rejection can be found in her girlhood. When she was in junior high school her good grades and high test scores enabled her to win a scholarship to a private girl's school. Her parents were thrilled that Miriam would have the opportunity to realize her potential. To please them and to keep her scholarship Miriam worked hard, got straight A's, and was miserable. Her classmates were so sure that she would raise the class curve on grading that they made a pact not to talk to her. By rejecting her they hoped to either make her leave or get her so rattled that her grades would suffer. For the next two years Miriam was left out of every party and social gathering at school. Her teachers were her only friends, so she worked harder to please them, and became even more unpopular with her peers. Miriam suffered in silence, never confiding her troubles to her parents or teachers, but the memories of those two years are as painful today as they were thirty years ago. And Miriam never plans to get in a position where her ability may cause her to be rejected again.

Being alone often accentuates and reinforces a woman's feeling that she's "no good." Many of us cherish solitude. We take stock of ourselves, plan new activities, and engage in our favorite pastimes. After all, if you're alone, there's nobody to please but yourself. You can spend the morning in a bubble bath, eat chocolates for breakfast, or stay up all night reading a new novel. "I look forward to my time alone," says one healthy career woman. "I'm able to go into myself and experience feelings that are often shut off during the business day. Being alone gives me time to answer the questions inside me instead of those of my staff and my family." This woman seeks solitude, but many women see being alone as the ultimate form of rejection. To be alone means that nobody wants to be with them. "I'll do anything to avoid being alone, even if it means joining groups that I don't really enjoy," says a woman whose calendar is jammed with meaningless activities.

When you're alone, you can either use the time constructively to grow and regroup, or you can use it negatively to retreat into destructive self-images. One woman may choose to shop alone because she prefers to make her decisions quickly and decisively without being hampered by another person's opinion, while another woman may shop alone because she doesn't think anybody wants to go with her. It's always wise to remember that you may do exactly the same thing that your best friend does, but for entirely different reasons.

You may also see rejection in incidents that have very different explanations. Amy was lunching in a crowded restaurant when she noticed a neighbor at a nearby table. She smiled and waved, but the woman ignored her. Lunch was spoiled for Amy; suddenly she felt rejected. Anxious to avoid another snub, Amy ignored her neighbor when she left the restaurant. How different the episode would have been if Amy had stopped by the table. She would have discovered that her neighbor had just been to the eye doctor, who had insisted that she remove her contact lenses for a week. Amy's friend could barely see the food on her plate, let alone the other side of the restaurant.

Not everybody responds to rejection the way Amy did. Some people adopt the *I Don't Think You're So Hot Either* response by discrediting the person who's rejected them, or by trying to negate or invalidate the rejection. In this approach, you decide that the boss who fires you for always being late is really a crook who ought to be fired himself; if you're turned down for a job because you lack typing proficiency you reply that it was a rotten job with terrible hours and no chance of advancement. You're simply covering up your feeling of worthlessness.

An *I Don't Think You're So Hot Either* approach will inhibit your growth and keep you from drawing honest conclusions about a situation. Sometimes those conclusions are painful, but often that's the only way we can grow.

Don't reject the other person, look at the rejection instead. If you're never included when your office mates go out for lunch, take a good look at yourself. Have you developed a cold exterior that makes people think you don't need them, all because you're afraid they may reject you? Do you belittle the very activities you'd like to be involved in?

Possibly you meet rejection with the *Armageddon* response. You turn a rejection into a catastrophic occurrence and act as if the world will come to an end by morning. When your boss tells you you're going to be laid off, you're convinced that nobody else will hire you and if you aren't working you'll lose your house and your car will be repossessed. One rejection—or even the *possibility* of one—and you're expecting the worst. Of course, it's possible that a disaster *will* occur, but you're going to be in a better position to deal with it if you wait for it to come to you instead of worrying yourself into such a panic that you become powerless.

———————•————

Now that you've looked at these three negative responses and

recognize the one *you* adopt, you can begin to deal constructively with rejection.

Separate the myth from the reality. Most likely it wasn't your
person, but your ideas, values, behavior, or opinions that were
rejected. Analyze the rejection so that you're absolutely sure
you know *what* was rejected. There are times when a woman's
low self-esteem, coupled with the unfamiliar world of the office, make her see rejection where it doesn't really exist. If your
boss tells you that a report or a memo needs work, do you accept that comment or do you decide that the whole report is
bad and if you wrote a bad report you must be a worthless
employee?

Once you give in to a feeling like this, you're apt to set
yourself up for failure by becoming dependent on your boss.
You ask his advice twice a day and check every report and
memo with him before you send it out. Eventually this kind of
behavior may cause you to be fired. An office is a place to get
company work done, it isn't a support system for your emotional hang-ups.

Remember that your company considers you a human resource. A newspaper editor explains it this way, "The paper
gets out every day because everybody from the typesetter to the
advertising department to the editors, reporters, and computer
operators has an individual job that they're responsible for.
There just isn't time to meet our deadlines if an employee needs
constant approval to get her job done."

Most businesses don't operate with the deadline pressure of
the morning press, but the principle remains the same. If you
become too dependent on your boss, you'll take away time that
he'd like to be spending on *his* job. And, sooner or later,
something will have to give. So try to deal with rejection
independently—and rationally.

You'll feel less rejected when an idea is criticized if you

remember two basic rules: don't assume anything more than what is said; and ask for feedback and clarification. Your boss always has the right to reject your work, and you always have the right to disagree with him. If you find that you're constantly disagreeing with him, you have the right *and* the responsibility to yourself to look for a different job that will be better suited to your talents.

———————

You can reverse rejection in your life by learning to define your *level of expectation*. Your level of expectation is the degree to which you expect certain things to happen; reality is what actually *does* happen. It's the gap between your level of expectation and reality that gets you into trouble and makes you feel depressed and rejected. If there isn't a very large gap between your level of expectation and reality, you aren't going to feel rejected or disappointed.

Schoolgirls spend hours debating the age-old question of which is better, anticipation or realization. Is thinking about the prom, the dress, and the corsage more fun than the prom itself? Often the dream cloud of expectation can wreck the real event and lead to disappointment. Nothing can match your fantasy.

When you anticipate, you control your make-believe world, but in reality you can't control other people's behavior. You don't know what they may do or why they may do it. Often you may be rejected for a reason that has nothing to do with you. A young woman in one of Florence's workshops told about writing a story about a boy growing up on a horse farm in the West. The story had recently appeared in a national magazine, but on an earlier submission to another magazine it had been rejected. Only later did the author discover that the editor who'd first turned down the piece had loathed horses.

Women just starting in the working world may have their level of expectation set too high. They see themselves becoming a duplicate of Mary Tyler Moore, with a super wardrobe, fascinating assignments, and long lunches with attractive people. Your reality is more likely to include long hours, boring office routine, tiredness, and a yearning to get back into a pair of jeans. No job is completely glamorous, or fun *all* the time, and as soon as you accept the fact that your job will involve chores as well as challenges, the gap between your level of expectation and reality will start to close.

You'll also get along better with your coworkers if you keep your level of expectation realistic. A common pitfall for many women, raised in the girlhood intimacy of best friends and slumber parties, is to try to find the same kind of relationships at the office. Fearful of being rejected, women immediately look for a best friend, never realizing that the person who offers friendship too quickly may just be suspect. She may want something back; she may feel left out herself and latch onto you to feel better about herself.

Helen discovered this the hard way. New and unsure of herself, she welcomed the help and friendship of a coworker who seemed only too eager to show her the ins and outs of the office, have lunch with her, and gossip about everybody in the company. After several weeks, Helen realized that her newfound Siamese twin was a gossip who had alienated everybody else in the office. She had no other friends, and Helen's relationship with her had also put Helen outside the main office group.

Be sure to allow yourself enough time to make a realistic assessment of any situation, both on the job and at home. Once you've spent six months in a new work or home community, you ought to be familiar enough with your new surroundings to adjust your level of expectation to suit them. At work it probably won't take as long. In a new job, you can also keep your level of expectation close to reality by having regular conferences with your boss. Whatever your job, you should plot your prospects by determining where you want to be and how you plan to get there—and then setting realistic goals.

Jane's story illustrates this point. Jane had enjoyed creative writing when she was in high school, but had never gone to college or taken a journalism course. Instead, she married and had four children. Her friends and family all enjoyed the marvelous letters she wrote.

When Jane was thirty-eight, her husband left her with the children and no particularly marketable skills. Once she had recovered from the initial shock, Jane began to set realistic levels of expectation for herself. Each time she met one she set a new one.

She started by taking the one thing she really enjoyed—writing—and turning it into a career. Her ultimate expectation was to write a book, but in reality it was going to take many small steps to reach that goal. If she had expected to write an immediate best-seller, the gap between her level of expectation and reality would have left her feeling rejected and depressed. Instead, she wrote a short article using the format of a letter to her children in which she reminisced about the years when they were growing up. She sent it to a national magazine, which promptly sent it back.

Jane admits that she felt horribly rejected when her story was returned. In fact, she buried it in her bureau drawer for a week. Then she adjusted her level of expectation and sent the story to a smaller magazine, which bought it and printed it. The story was picked up for reprint in a *second* magazine. Off and running, Jane wrote several more stories about her experiences as a mother, using either the letter or diary format, both of which were easy for her since she had been using them all her life.

Soon it was time to adjust her expectations again. She wanted to write about more than mothers and children, so she

applied for a job at a local newspaper. Never having had a journalism course, she knew that the odds were against her, but she
believed in herself and her ability to learn whatever she needed
to know—and she got the job. After working for a year on a
variety of subjects, Jane decided that she needed to have a
specialty. She asked to be assigned to the women's page because
she believed that women's issues were going to be making big
news.

After three years, Jane felt she was ready to write a book. She
prepared a proposal on a subject she had covered for the
paper—a job guide for teenagers—only to have it rejected by
ten publishers. After her disappointment, she again adjusted
her level of expectation. She saw that she needed to establish
more of a reputation for herself, so she left the local paper and
began selling articles to a national paper. "You have to keep
giving yourself a big push if you get too comfortable in a slot,"
she says.

After nine months of freelance writing, she sold an idea for
another book to a publisher. Jane will meet her original expectation of writing a book within the five-year time frame that she
originally allowed herself. She has done it by keeping each level
of expectation realistic and making regular readjustments.

Jane was realistic about her goals. You can't be realistic
about yours until you shatter your illusions, those false hopes
that you hang on to which have no basis in fact. For example, a
wife whose husband has been drinking for twenty-five years
may have the illusion that "someday he'll change." After
twenty-five years, the fact is that he drinks. She can either accept it and live with it or decide to leave him. Her expectations
must fit the reality of his drinking problem.

A common—and dangerous—illusion in the working world
is the notion that "If I do a really good job I'll get promoted and
get a raise." Maybe you will, but maybe you won't—in spite of
the good job you've done. And giving a lot of extra time to

your job doesn't guarantee you a promotion either.

For two years, Hope made her job at an engineering firm her life. She worked late every night, yet in spite of her devotion to her work and her loyalty to her boss she was the first employee to be fired when the firm lost a contract. Her boss was having an affair with his secretary, and the woman, who felt threatened by Hope, had been able to use her influence to make sure Hope was fired. Fifteen years later, Hope still feels that this rejection was somehow personal rather than political.

It may be wise to keep your level of expectation low when it's dependent on others, but you can make your *personal* level of expectation anything you want—the power to change yourself lies in your own hands. For example, you might decide to alter your personal style, to become less arrogant, suspicious, rigid, or unfeeling, and try to be more supportive of others, more self-confident or more optimistic. Maybe you have some bad habits you need to look at and change. Anything can happen when *you're* making the decision about yourself.

———————

You can strengthen your ability to deal with rejection by remembering a few basic concepts.

1. *Things change.* Change is a function of time. What's rejected today may be accepted tomorrow or next week. Of course, change can work the other way too. During the height of the space program, engineers were secure and well paid. When national priorities changed, cutbacks occurred throughout the industry and thousands of engineers found termination slips in their pay envelopes. Many men who were once engineers are now working in a variety of different capacities. Former engineers in one city were running an ice cream shop and a pizza parlor; operating a campground, a tire shop, and a produce store; and managing building projects. When inter-

viewed, these men admitted that they miss the excitement of their past life, but they also enjoy the rewards of the different lifestyles they lead now. Things had changed, and they had changed too. Even though you may not be forced into such a drastic career change, you should expect your working atmosphere to change as your company changes—with affirmative action programs, new environmental laws, and industrial health and safety guidelines.

2. *You change.* You change by getting older, and acquiring more experience and learning. An executive shared the following thoughts about his personal change: "When I was in my twenties, I wanted to travel anywhere and did at the drop of a hat. I was full of energy and excitement and thought I had to check out each project personally whenever there was a problem. Now, in my forties, I know that I'm not that important, and I'd rather stay home. I don't work more or less than I used to, but I do work smarter. Now I see the importance of quiet initial planning; before I used to shoot from the hip."

Social change is also responsible for individual change. For instance, a study of ten thousand Vassar alumnae who graduated in the mid-fifties found that they wanted marriage with or without a career. In the sixties, most wanted careers with or without marriage.

3. *Everything is relative.* In many cases, the success or failure of an interaction between two people depends on the situation, the time, the place, and how the people feel. A boss may reject *every* idea if he has a hangover or a personal problem. One woman who manages a crew of telephone linemen has noticed that her men reject her—and her orders—on days when they've been involved in hassles with their wives. By the same token, an editor may see promise in a new writer on a day when he's feeling good, but he may decide that he can't work with one more novice on a day when he's had a rough staff meeting.

4. *Don't put all your eggs in one basket.* In most cases, there's

more than one way to pursue a goal. For example, you may want a college degree but not have the money for tuition. You don't have to give up there. Many major corporations offer free college to their employees, so in order to reach your goal you might take a lower-level job in a corporation, go to school at night, and get a degree that will allow you to move to a better job. Never decide that you can't do something you want to do simply because you have the wrong kind of background.

Remember that nothing you do is wasted; all of your experiences can be made to fit into long-term objectives. If Jane had discovered that she needed more money than her newspaper job paid, she might have taken that valuable experience to get a job in public relations, a field with greater salary opportunities.

5. Realistically assess your capabilities, strengths, and weaknesses before you apply for a job. Often women set themselves up for rejection by applying for a job that requires skills they don't possess. The hunt-and-peck typist fails a typing test and immediately believes that her person as well as her typing has been rejected. The secretary applies for a job in a doctor's office, knowing that previous medical experience is required.

Naturally, there are exceptions. A woman with a healthy ego may apply for a job although she has none of the required skills, and, like Heather, she may get—and keep—it. Heather applied for a job as a legal secretary. Luckily, she didn't have to take a typing test because she couldn't type. Heather got the job—and spent the next three weekends teaching herself to type on her father's typewriter. Within a few weeks, she was good enough to manage on the job.

Remember that many of your skills from home can be adapted to the office. For example, if you've been handling all the family bookkeeping, you can easily learn to do the same at work. Women serve as comptrollers for a great many companies, both large and small. "Women have an attention to detail, coupled with a bird-dog approach, that allows them to handle budgets at home and at work," explains one executive. "The sums of money may be larger, but the technique is often the same."

If you enjoy giving parties and making people feel at home, you're a natural for a sales job. After all, a successful party takes the same intuitive understanding of people as a sale. If you've served on school and neighborhood committees, you've learned to delegate responsibility and to work in a group. On the other hand, if you enjoy doing projects around the house, you might consider one of the nontraditional jobs now available to women. A female railroad engineer recalls that she was always mechanically oriented. She preferred her brother's toys to her own. "I would hate sitting chained to a desk," she explains. "I love the freedom of my job, and I don't mind getting dirty."

6. Reconsider rejection. Changing your own thinking pattern is one of the best protections against feeling rejected. After all, rejection is nothing more than another person exercising their right to disagree—and you have the *same* right to agree or disagree. Rejection is part of a learning process, it can allow you to look more deeply into certain aspects of your behavior. If you've never been rejected, it only means that you've never had the guts to take a risk.

If you want to be a winner at work, you'll need to toughen up your business hide. "The woman who takes rejection of an idea personally is behaving in an unprofessional manner," says one personnel director. The key to success lies in remaining flexible, setting realistic goals, and remembering that rejection is simply another part of everyday life, *everybody's* everyday life.

CHAPTER 3

I Don't Know Why He Hired Me

———————•◄••►◄———————

Sally was hired as an assistant to the public relations director by the personnel manager of a small corporation. Her briefcase bulged with evidence of her qualifications, and the personnel manager, who chose her over many other applicants, considered himself lucky to have gotten her. Sally, on the other hand, was convinced that he had made a mistake. "I don't know why he hired me. I'm sure I'll be fired the minute he discovers how little I know," she told her friends. She spent the first month on the job in a state of nervous dread waiting to be found out.

Unusual? Not at all. Sally's feelings are echoed by thousands of women who, after batteries of psychological tests and extensive interviews, still believe that their hiring is a fluke. Many businesswomen come to Florence's fear workshops complaining of feelings of discomfort and uneasiness on the job. Since they can't find a reason for these feelings, they automatically assume that they're not good enough for the job.

The new female employee suffers from a whole bag of irrational fears. Of course, men have many similar fears, but the difference lies in the fact that society has never sanctioned the image of the fearful man. On the other hand, ever since the first woman screamed at a mouse, women have been expected to be fearful and in need of protection—and that kind of socialization creates special problems for women at work. But before we look at these common pitfalls facing working women—such as the fear of taking risks or making decisions, or the fear of making mistakes—we need to investigate the basic emotion and where it comes from.

There's nothing new about fear. The word "phobia," a psychiatric term for intense fear, comes from the Greek *Phobos*, the name of a god who spread fear to the enemy. A likeness of Phobos was placed on warriors' shields before they went into battle—one of the earliest forms of psychological warfare. Even today, you're in pretty good company if you suffer from phobias. Alfred Hitchcock is afraid of policemen, and Howard Hughes was afraid of germs. Albert Camus was phobic about driving a car, and Freud was fearful of travel. Irrational fear—or anxiety, as it is often called—cuts across all socioeconomic, intellectual, and sexual boundaries. Conservative statistics suggest that at least twenty million Americans suffer from severe anxiety.

Fear is one of the most potent and destructive of all emotions. It controls lives, makes us do things we don't want to do, and keeps us from doing what we want to do. Fear causes many women to accept jobs well below their capabilities; fear makes them remain in secretarial pools instead of taking advantage of companies' affirmative action programs. They're afraid of failure, afraid of making a mistake, and afraid of assuming new responsibility.

Many women are neither challenged by nor particularly happy in their jobs, but that's the price they pay for giving in to their fear. "I get so angry with our women workers," says an hourly placement officer at a steel mill. "The company opened up new opportunities for them, but they refuse to try something different."

Fear cripples, paralyzes, and lingers on. You'll never reach your full potential until you learn to break its grip. The first step is to understand what you're up against.

Fear may be either rational or irrational. Rational fear is a state of apprehension in the face of real danger. It's the way one of Florence's workshop participants felt as a nine-year-old child when she saw a bull approaching her mother, who was deaf. She ran across the field at an unbelievable speed, darted in front of the bull, and managed to successfully divert the enraged animal while her mother fled to safety. Later, nobody could believe that she had run that fast. Today she is fifty, but she still remembers every second of that afternoon. "As I ran, I felt stronger than I've ever felt since."

Several years ago, the newspapers carried the story of a young mother weighing just a hundred pounds who had lifted a car off the pinned body of her child. Like the girl in the previous story, she exhibited superhuman ability in a state of rational fear. Her body mobilized all of its forces to accomplish a feat of strength that would have been impossible under normal conditions.

Many of us are not as effective as she was in confronting rational fear. We may freeze and be unable to move or even think. If you fall into this category, you can alter your behavior by using the eight-point fear program at the end of this chapter.

The woman who lifted the car from the body of her child and Sally, our panicky public relations director, both experienced a physical reaction in which fear, either real or imagined, triggered the body's sympathetic nervous system. Signals like this were essential to our forefathers' survival. Whether our early ancestors decided to fight or flee when danger threatened, they needed additional strength. Adrenalin poured into their bodies to increase their energy, their pupils dilated to sharpen their vision, their salivary glands were inhibited from functioning so their mouths became dry, their sweat glands overreacted to produce clammy hands and a cold sweat. Their hearts were stimulated, and their breathing accelerated. The name of the game was survival.

Twentieth-century life patterns have changed, but the human body has not. It doesn't distinguish between life-and-death situations and simply daily frustrations. Your fear may be of making mistakes, of not being liked, or of being fired—but your body still reacts as if you were facing a life-threatening danger. This is irrational fear, the fear of an *imagined* danger. It is always debilitating and self-limiting until you identify its source and conquer the fear.

The basic physiological response to fear is automatic, but most researchers believe that fears are learned. The classic experiment in this area was that performed on "Little Albert" by Dr. John Watson, one of the pioneers of behavioral psychology. Eleven-month-old Albert was shown a furry white rat while he played in his crib. Initially, he was unafraid of the animal, but when a loud noise began to accompany the rat's appearance he soon became afraid of the animal. The feared noise was associated with the sight of the rat. Even after the noise was dropped from the experiment he continued to fear the rat. His fear generalized, and soon he was afraid of other white objects, furry objects, and even a man's beard. This experiment provided researchers with clinical proof not only that fear is learned, but that when a feared object is paired with a neutral one the person learns to fear the neutral object.

It's easy to learn fear. One lesson may be all you need—and the effects of that fear may be far-reaching and difficult to reverse. A remarkable number of women who attend Florence's workshops fear the loud male voice. In these women's subconscious, the loud male voice is associated with the fear of punishment from their father. Years later when they're on the job, they replay techniques learned in childhood for dealing with that fear.

Debbie is an assistant account executive with a large advertising company. During a workshop she confessed that although she came to staff meetings full of new and innovative ideas she was unable to speak up the minute the men raised their voices. Instead, she shrank back into her chair and remained silent until prodded. As a little girl, Debbie had learned that the best way to please her father when he was angry was to be very good and very quiet until he wanted to speak to her. Women like Debbie are often not aware that they fear the loud male voice. Instead they think they're afraid of their boss, or of staff meetings.

It's difficult to accept the fact that in many cases the people who wanted the best for you—your parents—may have been responsible for teaching you some of the fears that stunt your growth and limit your potential. It was not a deliberate act; in many cases your fears develop by following the example of a parent's own immature and fearful behavior. The parent who reacts to the problems of daily life with fear or panic is unconsciously teaching a child the same kind of behavior.

Your parents believed that they were insuring your safety when they warned you against talking to strangers. They feared the child molester, so they told you, "Don't talk to strangers" or "Don't trust people who are nice to you if they aren't Mommy's friends." So the young child learns that all strangers are bad and to be feared. She does not forget that early warning, but her fear generalizes. As an adult she discovers that she's uneasy and uncomfortable whenever she must meet new people. She gets a knot in her stomach before a cocktail party or breaks out in a cold sweat before making a presentation to people she doesn't know. This happens to men as well as to women.

Paul was a strapping, muscular young man of twenty-five. His job involved a great deal of travel, yet he felt panicky whenever he arrived in an airport late at night—even if all he had to do was take a taxi to his hotel. Certainly his fear was not rational. Built like a weight lifter, he could have decked any wallet snatcher with one hand.

As Florence looked into his past history, she discovered one incident that had generalized. When Paul was seven he took the train home from school. A teacher walked him and his classmates to the station and his mother met him at the other end. Then one day he stayed too long at school and not only missed the group but also the train. He was alone in the station. In tears, he called his mother.

Instead of calmly alleviating his anxiety, she increased his fear because she was fearful herself. "Don't talk to anybody; just wait there. No, don't get another train; it might be going somewhere else. I'll come and pick you up." So seven-year-old Paul sat and waited, frightened of the station and frightened of being alone and frightened of any transportation but Mother. At twenty-five he was still waiting for his mother to pick him up at the airport.

Understanding the original fear often helps us to get rid of its present manifestations. Sheila came to a fear workshop because she had difficulty making friends. Her husband was a corporate executive, and they had moved a number of times—but she was still unable to trust new people when she met them. "I'm always thinking about what they want from me," she explained. By the time she was ready to be a friend she had usually succeeded in alienating her new neighbors. As Florence traced her fear backward, Sheila remembered a long-forgotten incident. In the first grade, a classmate had been molested by an older man who had worked in the local drugstore, a man who was always friendly with the children and gave them free candy. Her mother was unable to discuss the incident with her. All she could manage was to sit her down at the kitchen table and give her this advice, "I never want you to forget what I'm about to say. People aren't the way they seem. If a strange person is friendly, get away as fast as you can. It's not safe to be friendly." Sheila had been reacting to her new neighbors as if they were those strangers her mother had warned her about.

———————•◆•———————

All of us have fears, but the difference between a happy and fulfilled life and a threatened existence lies in the way you deal with those fears. You can conquer your fear by practicing a few simple exercises.

Learn to identify your fears. Recognize the feeling of discomfort and tension the minute it arises. What are you doing? Trace the feeling back, step by step, until you arrive at the source. *That* is your fear. You may need to do this several times before you're quite sure—sometimes you think you're afraid of one thing when actually your fear is of something else entirely. For instance, fear of failure may be fear of somebody else's disapproval. Fear of giving an opinion may be fear of looking stupid. Fear of making a mistake may be fear of not being liked. Fear of being fired may be fear of being broke or unable to find another job.

Once you have identified your fear, determine whether it's rational or irrational. Test its strength by testing your body's physical reaction. Learn to dissect your fear, familiarize yourself with it so that it won't sabotage you. An unidentified irrational fear will consume your productivity, while a known fear becomes a fact that you can deal with.

Judy came to a fear workshop because she felt nervous and anxious on days when she had to mail her boss's letters. She counted and recounted the letters before dropping them in the slot. Once she mailed them she felt fine. Why was Judy afraid to mail letters? She dissected her fear and remembered that as a little girl she used to mail letters for her mother—and one snowy day she had lost her father's mortgage payment on the way to the mailbox. At thirty-two she is sabotaged by a long-forgotten childhood experience.

When fear becomes familiar you're in a position to desensitize yourself. In a case like Judy's, it may be enough to simply understand the origin of the fear, but in others you may need to increase your knowledge of it. For example, you may be afraid of speaking up at meetings. You can begin to desensitize yourself by talking first to one person at a meeting, then expanding it to two or three. Each time you complete a conversation or discuss an idea, you're substituting action for fear. Soon you'll be addressing the whole group.

After you have familiarized yourself with your fear, learn how you've been coping with it in the past. Many fearful people avoid facing the fear directly. They take trains rather than deal with their fear of flying. They avoid a fearful event by getting sick. Some people avoid a fear by becoming aggressive. The woman who is afraid to meet new people may avoid her fear by saying, "Everybody I meet these days is so dull. I prefer having just one or two good friends."

You'll be able to hang up the fear habit as soon as you strengthen your own thinking process by using this eight-step program:

STEP 1: *Sizing Up.* Often fear makes people distort reality. When you experience fear, take hold of your environment and interpret it accurately instead of simply giving in to your fears. Mobilize all your thinking power so you see things as they really are.

STEP 2: *Personal Potency.* Fear causes us to feel helpless, a throwback to the childhood years when we were dependent on our parents for survival. You're not helpless now, and you don't need your parents' approval or support for the things you choose to do. Your personal potency allows you many options in any situation. Review them.

STEP 3: *Share Your Fear.* Fears diminish when they're shared. Find a supportive friend and talk about your fear. Many people keep the fear habit going by holding it in and telling themselves that they shouldn't be afraid. Accept your fear as a temporary part of yourself that you plan to change.

STEP 4: *Shrink Your Fear.* Frequently, an object of fear is imbued with omnipotent and magical powers. Put your fear into realistic perspective. Your boss is only your boss in this job, and this job is only one of many you may hold. All he can do is fire you. If you choose to leave, you'll have another boss in another job.

STEP 5: *Wipe Out Worry.* Worry drains your psychic energy and gives you nothing in return. It's a useless feeling with no place in your life. The way you approach each situation affects the way it will turn out. So give up worry binges and concentrate on positive, constructive thoughts that will reduce your fears. Change worry to action.

STEP 6: *Set Realistic Goals.* You'll experience many setbacks in your life, but they won't be as difficult to deal with if your goals are realistic ones. Total competence at all times is unrealistic. You can't be a perfect mother, wife, employee, or boss. Rearrange your goals in a workable, attainable framework.

STEP 7: *Make a Plan.* Decide who you need to call on for help with your fear and how much information you need about the fear. Then draw up a plan, setting daily goals for overcoming your fear. Break the fear habit by facing fears gradually, a little at a time.

STEP 8: *Do It.* Take control of your life. You're the driver, not the passenger. Rid yourself of negative interferences, strengthen your positive thinking process, estimate the probability of events, and be prepared to deal with them. START TODAY.

CHAPTER *4*

Decisions, Risks, and Mistakes

———————————

Women have more options than they've ever had before. They have the freedom to choose a personal lifestyle, a career, and educational goals, but many of them don't have the ability to make these decisions rationally. Why? Because having a choice means taking a risk—and a risk always involves the possibility of failure. And that's something a lot of women can't bear to think about.

A great many women in today's work force have been raised according to the philosophy that women should be seen and not heard. They expect their fathers and later their husbands to make most of the really important decisions in their lives. "I remember my mother telling each of us that all we had to do was worry about finding a man," said one workshop participant. "After that all the decisions would be up to him."

Traditionally, men have decided how much money to spend on a house, when to buy a car, and where to go on vacation, while women decided on the inconsequential aspects of daily living—what to have for dinner, which movie to see, and where to go for cocktails. The social expectations of the female role allow them these decisions, and decisions about the children, but hardly ever financial ones. Women in the office often continue this "housekeeping" view of decision-making. They're apt to be more concerned about regulating the office supplies than they are with considering the far-reaching and at times risky parameters of the job. They think about the appearances and not the substance.

Sheila was hired as a project manager and given a four hundred and fifty thousand dollar budget. She'd been a homemaker for many years, and wasn't used to putting a value on her own time. "I cheated my boss out of my executive thinking and planning time by spending hours trying to save my department nickels and dimes," she remembers. "I might have continued if he hadn't taken me aside and pointed out that he hadn't hired me just to save him money on a copying machine."

As a helpmate to her husband, a woman is used to listening to him think out his decision—but she's not used to doing the same thing on her own. A woman who later became an executive with an insurance company puts it this way, "I had helped my husband with his choices for years, but I was really frightened when I was doing it for myself. Then *I* was responsible for the consequences."

Whether or not you realize it, you're making decisions every day. And when you come right down to it, *not* making a decision is, in it's own way, also a kind of decision. Doris shared this story with a recent workshop. After deciding that she wanted a serious career as a writer she set out to order some business stationery—but she fled the store in a panic after only half an hour of vascillating between different shades of grey, cream, and white stock. By not choosing she had made a decision to postpone her purchase—and maybe her career.

Women are not yet comfortable in a decisive position because their early training has been as followers and deferers. Their desire to make other people feel better keeps them from choosing what *they* want.

As a teenager you probably went along with the crowd. Your only independent decisions dealt with make-up, hair, and clothing. You let your date choose the evening's entertainment because you didn't want to choose something he wouldn't like. This same kind of behavior is translated to the office, where it can get you into big trouble.

Barbara's boss asked her to tell him when her report on a new product would be available. Instead of making a decision, she shifted the responsibility to him by asking, "When do you need it?" She was trapped when he said that he needed it in two days. Barbara copped out on decision-making a second time when she accepted her boss's time frame and didn't tell him she might need several more days to finish. Instead, she complained to everybody at the office that her boss always wanted everything done yesterday, when in fact the fault was *hers*, not his. She could easily have told her boss that the report would be finished the following week. If that was too late for his needs, they could have worked out another schedule together.

If you don't make a decision, somebody else will make it *for* you, and their decision for your life may come back to haunt you. "I thought I wanted to have a career, but my mother was so anxious for me to get married and be safe that I accepted her decision about my life and married a man I didn't love," says a woman who only realized her goal many years later, following a divorce.

Some women find it difficult to take an action without the approval of others; they still have to learn that business decisions cannot be approached like popularity contests. The project manager for a new office building used the following story to illustrate this point. His construction deadline had been set for January, and meeting that deadline required him to make a great many unpopular decisions and to be accused of ignoring proposals from some of the department heads who would be occupying the building. However, he knew that if he tried to please each department and made all the changes they wanted he wouldn't meet his deadline and the company would go over their budget for the project. Each of his decisions was determined by his consideration of the bottom line, and although he ruffled some feathers along the way, in the end he was commended for his performance.

Obviously, good decisions are ones in which the skills of decisionmaking are used to choose the best alternative. Since it's the individual who makes the decision, it's always wise to remember that a good decision for you may be a bad one for another person. Making a change in jobs or opting for a career over marriage may be right for one woman but completely wrong for another. Oddly enough, says a college counselor, many of today's young women cope with an inner conflict over wanting to get married when they think they "ought" to have a career.

All of Tammy's career decisions had been easy, including a major switch from research scientist to personnel consultant. Then, at age thirty, she fell in love with a man who wanted her to follow him to Germany, where he had an excellent job offer. "Usually I can tell by my gut feeling what I want to do," she said, "but this time I just avoided discussing our future plans. I didn't know what to do. I *did* know that a wrong decision usually takes more time for me to make—so if I'm deliberating too long it's a pretty good clue."

Tammy decided to keep her job, and her friend then took a different job which allowed him to stay in the country six months longer. Tammy made her decision after weighing her relationship and her career. Hers was an aggressive career choice, not unlike the ones that men have been making for years—but the kind of choice that's relatively new to women.

Her decision was made more easily because she didn't see it as irrevocable. "I used to think my decisions were permanent, and I felt locked in by them. Now I know that if I make one decision that isn't right I can always make another one. The only *bad* thing is to do nothing."

Successful decision-making comes from following your internal feelings about yourself. Nobody else knows you as well— and nobody else will have to live with your decision. In many cases, you'll find that you have a flash feeling of what decision you *want* to make, but instead you push it away and do something quite different *and* quite wrong.

Subliminal information is always there as an available resource for you to tap, but you may need to learn how to get in touch with it. You might start by keeping a diary of your immediate feelings in different situations. Did you choose to act on them or did you do something else? If you chose somebody else's decision, or did something because you thought you ought to, did it prove to be right or wrong in the long run? Checking your weekly decision guide will teach you to make the kinds of decisions you *really* want to make.

Once you've made a decision, it's often your parents who are the hardest to please and who try the hardest to veto your choice. You have options today that would have been beyond the realm of possibility or probability for your mother. You don't have to sit at a desk or behind a stack of files for the day if you prefer working with your hands. However, your choice to take a nontraditional job—to be a carpenter, a plumber, or a mortician—may bring you into an open, hostile confrontation with your parents, who still believe that being a wife and mother are the proper slots for a woman.

"My father believed in two jobs for women—secretary or airline stewardess—so you can imagine his horror when I told him I wanted to be a plumber," recalls a young woman who participated in a CETA training program for women in non-traditional jobs. "My mother just cried that she hadn't raised me to work in strangers' bathrooms." A mother whose daughter announced that she was going to be a mortician recalls feeling dismayed and ashamed. "My social self-esteem collapsed. How could I possibly admit my daughter's chosen profession to my friends? What would they think of me?"

Bess, the mother of five and the daughter of very traditional Hungarian parents, remembers her father's outright hostility when she decided to be a carpenter. "My Dad used to boast about the way I made repairs on the family house, but he hit the roof when I decided that I wanted to be paid for what I enjoyed doing. Luckily, my husband was supportive, but it was still a tough transition because I had to cope with both my father's hostility and the hostility of the men on the job. At first I thought about giving up, but I'm glad I stuck with it." Today she's making $7 an hour in her nontraditional job—and an added bonus is her influence on her daughter's view of a woman's role. When her child's kindergarten teacher asked her to circle the objects that she associated with a mother, she chose an iron, a stove, and a saw!

Helen is another woman who has chosen a nontraditional field. She spent three years taking pre-med courses in college before realizing that she really wanted a hands-on mechanical career. "I've always loved working with machines, but I didn't think it was very feminine," she explains. When Helen dropped out of college, much to her parents' dismay, she explained that she couldn't justify taking any more of their money for a career she didn't want. Instead, she enrolled in a five-month electronics program and is now employed by an electronics firm which will pay for her additional schooling. She's also making more money than her plumber husband.

Decisions, Risks, and Mistakes

Some women make poor decisions because they act too quickly, without weighing all their alternatives. Cindy, a recent engineering school graduate, was offered a starting salary of $21,000 a year by a company in her home town. The thought of making such an incredible salary as a 22-year-old woman led her to accept the job immediately. She didn't think the decision through. If Cindy had taken another job at a lower salary that had been offered her by an oil company, she could have realized her dream of travel and expanded her personal horizons. As a single woman she didn't really need a salary of $21,000 a year, and the safe job in her home town was going to be limiting in spite of the salary.

Before you make a decision, you need to examine *every* possible alternative. At work you may need to consult a number of people to get all the information you need. And these people may suggest additional alternatives. One woman executive says that she's always disappointed if she takes a problem to her boss and he agrees with her proposed solution. "Two brains should be better than one!" is her rationale.

Remember that a good decision is based on all the available information you have *at the time that you make it.* At a future time, you may have more information and may decide to make a *different* decision. A decision is good because of the *way* that it's made not because of how it turns out. You can't expect to predict future events that may result. For example, you might decide to buy a home close to your children's elementary school. Two years later, the school is closed and your kids are bused to a school in another town. Do you spend a lot of time blaming yourself, saying, "We should never have bought this house," or do you accept the fact that it was a good decision when you made it, but that things have changed since then? If you're smart, you'll remember that if a good decision results in a bad turn of affairs, all you have to do to correct things is make *another* good decision.

———— •—•————

Kate brought this problem to a decision workshop. She was married and working full time. Her house never seemed tidy because she disliked spending her Saturdays cleaning. Her husband was bothered by the mess, but didn't offer to help. Kate complained about this and remarked that he seemed to think his job was more important than hers. Feelings about whose job was more important appeared to be only red herrings in the housecleaning issue. But as Kate considered her options— forcing her husband to help, leaving the house a mess, or hiring help—she realized that her feelings about her job were the real reason she had delayed making a decision. Once she understood that, she had no trouble deciding to hire someone to help out.

Like Kate, some women appear to enjoy playing the martyr, and they refuse to make a decision that will ease their situation. If you find that you have too many good reasons or "yes, buts" about why a problem can't be solved, it's likely that you don't *want* to make a change. You may be using a real situation to vent a lot of unrelated feelings. In Kate's case, those feelings had to do with her self-worth, the question of whose job was more important. Take a look at your red herrings. Have you addressed them directly or do you piggyback them onto another issue?

———— •—•————

Making a decision may require giving an order, and women often fear giving orders because they believe they'll be labelled pushy, aggressive, or unfeminine. When Mary was hired as the project director of a rehabilitation program, she was eager to be liked. She had a professional staff of six to whom she gave orders in a nice, gentle voice, liberally lacing her requests with "Do you mind" and "Would you please." Nobody listened and nothing got done. Nobody took her seriously because she didn't seem to take herself seriously. She admits that she thought of herself as "Who me? The administrator?" until she looked around and saw all the work that needed to be done. She forgot about being popular when she realized that she might be fired. She discovered that the minute she began making firm decisions without worring about being liked, her staff began working instead of taking advantage of her. And she discovered that they liked her better because she'd become a better administrator.

Many women who've been pushed into new positions to satisfy affirmative action programs simply aren't equipped for the decisions they'll have to make to succeed in their new jobs. These women accept new titles or fancier offices without asking any questions. Like traditional submissive females, they defer to their superiors and feel grateful for any benefits that come their way.

Linda had been secretary to the boss of a packaging firm for years. When the company received a government contract, Linda was given the new title of Assistant Marketing Director and an office with a sofa and a coffee table, along with a salary boost. Local newspapers showed pictures of the new executive sitting at her desk, and Linda, enjoying the supposed glamour of her job, expected that she'd be right in on the company decision-making. That bubble of expectation burst after several months when she realized that in spite of the new office and the new title, she had the same responsibilities as before. Like many women, Linda had just waited for things to happen *to* her. Because she didn't have the decision-making skills to make something of her new position, she simply made the best of her old job in her new surroundings.

—•—

If you're having difficulty making important decisions, you'll need to build your decision-making skills (*and* your confidence) in small ways, starting with yourself. Begin practicing at home by having an opinion *whenever* you're asked for one, even on the most trivial subjects. Try taking the opposing position when a discussion is going on. Remember too that a decision often requires you to take some form of *action*. Many people substitute thought or talk for action.

You can strengthen your decision-making skills at work by seeking out situations that will give you practice. For example, if you know your boss is planning to buy a copier, you might ask to research the different brands and submit an opinion. Gathering information about different kinds of machines— their price, their performance, and their guarantee—is the same as weighing alternatives—and writing a memo detailing your findings and suggestions is the same as making a decision. It doesn't matter if your boss doesn't take your recommendation—all that *you* can control is *your* ability to make it.

--------•--------

Many decisions involve taking risks, yet many women have been trained to prefer a safe situation. When you were a child, it's likely that you were protected by your mother, cautioned against going out alone, warned about the risks of climbing a tree or a roof, and considered to be more fragile, more apt to get hurt either emotionally or physically, than the boys in the family. When such protected little girls arrive on the business scene they have little or no experience in bending the rules or taking a risk.

A woman's inherent need to do it by the book automatically limits her potential. The spice and adventure of business come from taking risks. Anybody who has sat through a one-sided game at the ball park will agree that a safe game can be *very* dull. If you develop a reputation for being very cautious, you may discover that the exciting jobs aren't given to you.

Being willing to take a risk may change the whole scope of your life. For example, you and your husband may be working in your home town, close to all your family support groups. Suppose he's offered a better job halfway across the country. It certainly is a risk to move, to pull up stakes and chart a new course for yourself in an area where you have neither family nor friends. But if you take the risk and make the decision to move, you may have many new and challenging experiences.

Sometimes you may want to make a decision but decide against it because the risk is *too* great. A man may yearn to have his own business, but may feel that he can't give up the security of a corporate job because of his family obligations. So he decides not to take a risk. In his case, it's a wise decision, but there are many *other* cases in which men and women make up a variety of reasons for remaining in safe, protected positions simply because they're afraid. A steel company executive notes that women often choose not to take advantage of opportunities for new jobs at higher salaries. Says a shift worker at the same plant, "I know I could be a crane operator and double my salary, but I don't know what to expect. I don't want all that uncertainty. I'm not happy where I am, but at least I *know* what I'm not happy about."

Early socialization has trained women to be passive family members instead of initiators. A woman is trained to wait for things to happen *to* her—for a husband to choose her, and then for her subordinate role in the family. It's no wonder that many women lack confidence in their ability to make independent choices. They prefer to be "prepared and safe" rather than adventurous. Such an attitude has to have an impact on a woman's job performance.

A group of women were hired by an electronics company to work on a contract job. As the project neared completion, all the women but one began to worry about being laid off. Naturally, their job performance was affected. Vera was the exception; she continued to work at her top capacity. She was convinced that she would get another job with the company, particularly if her supervisor gave her a good recommendation. "My father taught us that life was one big adventure and we could have anything we wanted," she explains. "All we have to do is take the risk and reach." She was too busy working to worry about being laid off, and she was the only member of the crew to be kept on after the job was finished.

Taking risks enables many men to get ahead because the risk-carrying positions are also the high visibility ones. According to Hennig and Jardim's *The Managerial Woman*, men see a risk as a win-or-lose proposition, while women tend to think only about the danger of losing. "I don't want to jeopardize my future with the company by sticking my neck out," says a woman who may never move from supervisor to manager. "If I go out on a limb, I'm sure somebody will decide to prune the tree."

On the other hand, women may become zealous crusaders at work and may take foolhardy risks to change company policies. One executive used this example: "For years our company bought all of its lighting fixtures from one supplier. Then a new woman manager suddenly began complaining and checking out prices; she insisted that we dump our supplier and she was very vocal about it. Maybe she was right, but in the end *she* was dumped. The supplier turned out to be the president's cousin, and by the time she found out it was too late to cover her tracks." Taking this kind of a risk is a sign of ignorance, not a sign of strength.

————— •·• —————

If you lack confidence in your ability to take risks, you may need to build yourself up in the same way you do when you're learning to make decisions—by starting in very small ways. Small successes in each new behavior pattern give you the confidence to take larger risks and make more important decisions, just the way your first steps lead to the ability to jog two miles.

Start by taking a few personal risks such as saying hello to a stranger at.a party or giving your boss an opinion that he didn't ask for—or even disagreeing with him. Keep the issue small— say, giving him an opinion of an article you've read—but pay attention to how he responds if he disagrees with you and how you feel in the same situation. Do you cave in? These small beginnings lead to taking larger risks, such as being able to make a comment in a meeting.

Beth was frightened of taking personal risks at the office, so she decided to practice at church. She'd attended the same church for years but left directly after the service and knew very few members of her congregation. She forced herself to stay for the coffee hour and to speak to one new person each Sunday. The first few weeks were difficult, but she remembers with joy the day she spoke to an extra person simply because she *wanted* to, not because she *had* to. Soon Beth had signed up for a committee, and now she proudly serves on her church vestry. She is as at home with her office mates today as she is with her church congregation.

Another way to improve your risk-taking behavior at work is to find one aspect of your job that you'd like to change. For example, plan to change your filing system. Write a memo to your boss telling him that you're going to redesign the system, explaining why, and providing a date when you'll be finished. If he doesn't veto the idea, go ahead and *do* it. When you're finished, write him a memo telling him the system is complete. In doing this, you're taking a good, small risk which will gain the attention of your boss, and self-esteem for yourself. Each time you initiate a small risk, you'll find you gain the personal strength to try another. Keep taking risks, and don't worry if they don't *always* work out. Taking a risk means that you're willing to try a new kind of behavior.

———————•—•———————

Women are often afraid to take risks because they're afraid of making a mistake. It doesn't matter whether you're a manager, a waitress, or a telephone installer—you're going to make mistakes because you're *human*. Despite this obvious truth, many women can't bear the thought of making a mistake. They don't realize that a mistake is simply an unplanned learning experience.

An unreasonable fear of making a mistake may be traced back to parents who set unrealistic expectations for you. Many parents live through their children and believe that the perfect child is in fact nothing more than a reflection of a perfect mother or father. The child in this kind of a family grows up believing that she must do everything better if she's going to be loved and accepted. She may be punished for getting a B on a report card, but she's never rewarded for getting an A because an A is expected. When this child becomes an adult, she'll probably derive very little satisfaction from each business success or promotion, and she'll equate even a small error with failure.

The common fear involved in making a mistake is the belief that an error will make people think less of you. And you were absolutely correct about that back in elementary school. Remember those jeers about being dumb on a spelling test or muffing a catch at third base? Well, it's time to reverse the fear gear and remind yourself that school is *over*. Everybody makes mistakes. Every member of the working world, from the typist to the chairman of the board, is confronted with their own mistakes and inefficiencies.

All a mistake means is that you had the courage to try something and haven't succeeded yet. Learn from your mistake. See what you did wrong and correct it.

The most important part of learning to deal with a mistake is to admit that you *made* one—and this is where many women get into trouble. Women in management often feel that they're on display, looked at more carefully than the men in the office. "I feel as if my coworkers are waiting for me to make just *one* mistake," says a woman manager who's new to her position. "I'm on my mettle to prove myself every day. The men I work with aren't liberated, and they honestly believe that I'm taking the food out of another man's mouth. I feel as if they *want* me to fail." Because these women feel under such pressure to be perfect, they often try to cover up their mistakes. If you admit a mistake, it's done with, but when you try to hide it you can get into even more trouble.

A manager explains it this way, "When I started in my new job I covered my mistakes by making them look like correct choices. The problem was that I kept having to defend actions that I didn't believe in. Today it's much easier just to say I made a mistake. Nobody's going to do anything to me because everybody else makes them too."

A personnel consultant admits that in the past she was apt to get upset and defensive over making an error. Recently she made a mistake in bypassing a vice president who should have been consulted about a decision. "He scheduled a conference with me, explained the severity of my mistake, and levelled with me. For the first time, I was able to see him as my coach and not as my parent. I appreciated his help and agreed with him about my error. *That* is growth for me."

Admitting a mistake gives you an opportunity to learn new ways of dealing with a situation. It becomes a positive resource when you can look at it as a new tool for future growth. For example, Frances was asked to prepare a department evaluation for her boss. She started with the departments with which she was the most familiar and saved the complex ones till the end. When an unexpected office emergency occurred, she had to put the job aside for awhile. When she picked it up again, she was behind schedule, and the most difficult part of the job still remained. From this experience, Frances learned to organize herself differently the next time she had a similar assignment. Since all offices have unexpected crises, it made more sense for her to *start* with the difficult part of the job and save the easy part until the end. Her mistake has provided her with an invaluable working system for the future. She could have lost that insight if she had spent all her time simply blaming herself for being inefficient.

Admit your mistake and learn from it, but don't dwell on it. In many cases, it helps to take a tip from the men in the office, who use the collective "we" when admitting a mistake—"We tried and we lost"—just the way they might over a baseball game. The team feeling diffuses that overall sense of failure. That important "we" feeling is not as strong for women, who've been socialized to feel *personally* responsible for everything. After all, a woman considers it *her* fault if her marriage fails or if her child gets into trouble. In contrast, male support systems involve *group* thought, action, and feeling. Nobody singles out the man who makes the final out and says that it's *his* fault the team lost. You're going to feel better about yourself at the office as soon as you can adopt that kind of philosophy.

One way to avoid mistakes is to make sure office procedures are consistent. Inconsistency results in ambiguity and ambiguity leads to error. Too often the manager who discovers mistakes in her department assumes that her *own* mistake lay in not doing *all* the work herself. But the real issue is that the goals, responsibilities, and relationships in her department weren't clearly established. Setting up basic procedures and clarifying the chain of command enables routine work to be handled smoothly and crises to be spotted and dealt with before they get out of control. Whether you're a boss or a subordinate, you'll make fewer mistakes if you know exactly what's expected of you.

On the other hand, there's always the possibility that you may be fired for making too many mistakes on the job, for a personality conflict with your boss—or even simply because of a shortage of work. Whatever the reason, men and women agree that getting fired temporarily shatters their self-esteem. They feel inadequate. But in many cases the failure at work that leads up to being fired may point up a deficiency or help you to determine a different attitude or interest. Failure isn't fun—but it isn't the end of the world either. You don't have to adopt a Pollyanna attitude about things that go wrong; just be honest enough to figure out how and why they *really* happened.

Once you've accepted the fact that you're going to make mistakes, and once you're determined to learn from them, you'll be in a position to profit from even your biggest disappointments. Although it may not seem so at the time, a failure *can* be a positive thing. One woman remembers that being fired from a job meant she could go on unemployment and take the remaining college credits for her teaching certificate. She passed, and got a job at an elementary school, which was where she had wanted to work all along.

An editor at a publishing house who wrote short stories in her spare time never considered herself a real writer until she was fired and had to write full-time. She has now published three novels.

Once you are able to accept your right to make mistakes and not be afraid of failure you'll be able to take the risks and make the decisions that are part of the business adventure. If you make a decision, take a risk, and win, you'll skyrocket to the top. And even if you lose, you can take consolation from the fact that you're still one step ahead of the women who've never stopped cowering in the corner.

CHAPTER 5

The Criticism Crumble

———————————

Your boss criticizes your work, your husband criticizes your housekeeping, your friend criticizes your dress. And each time the critic's words lie in your stomach like a 45-caliber bullet while you look for a hole to climb into, a bed to crawl under, or a cover to pull up over your head. In other words, criticism makes you feel miserable. You crumble.

When describing the effects of criticism, women often use phrases like, "I couldn't cope," "I fell apart," or "I felt frozen." One critical comment may paralyze a woman. Even a successful account executive can admit, "If my boss criticizes the way I handle a client, I can't function properly for the rest of the day."

Criticism is a normal part of daily life, but for many women it becomes a psychic stab that triggers an emotional instead of an intellectual response. Criticism is difficult to deal with because most of us need approval, and we interpret criticism as rejection or disapproval. If your early training and socialization taught you to be a polite, pretty people-pleaser who accommodates and acquiesces you'll be more susceptible to criticism than a man. You think in terms of popularity while a man thinks in terms of respect.

Of course approval is nice to have, but you'll survive without it as long as you're meeting standards that are acceptable to you. It's neither possible nor realistic to please everybody, so concentrate on pleasing your only constant companion—YOU.

The bonus for this behavior is liking yourself because you're doing what you believe to be right. Other people may not like you, but they'll respect you. "The more I work and observe the really successful executives, men and women," says one prominent woman executive, "the more I'm convinced that the old virtue of integrity—the willingness to stand up and be counted for what you believe is right—is an absolute must."

———————————

Criticism is often based on somebody else's value system or judgment of how you should act in certain situations, so understanding your critic's value system will make you better able to deal with criticism. Remember that a person who's older or younger than you are will often have a different value system. For example, imagine that you're a woman in your forties working for a man in his thirties. He might expect you to treat him as a coworker, while you're probably tempted to slip into a maternal role and expect him to be a respectful son—and so you're apt to resent his criticism. After all, you've been around longer than he has, and from your perspective some of his comments may seem impertinent—his criticism has become a threat to your ego. It can even be worse when your boss is a younger woman.

If your boss is older than you are, he or she is apt to expect deferential and possibly submissive behavior from an employee. This can cause friction with younger people, who tend to be more assertive and more willing to stand up for their rights. Whatever the situation, the important thing to remember is that an understanding of your critic will always help you to find the best way of dealing with him.

The Criticism Crumble

Most of us harbor several false assumptions about our critics. We often believe that a critic is correct and that his criticism represents a valid, true description of the state of affairs. But we didn't start out that way. Elementary school playgrounds ring with the shout, "Look who's talking," but by adult life we sometimes lose the valuable technique of seeing behind the critic's facade. When your coworker says that it takes you too long to type a letter, do you ask her how long is long? Or longer than whom? Probably not. You assume that she's right and you're wrong.

We also assume that critical blows to our fragile egos are the right of the critic. When your best friend tells you that you're neglecting your children because you've decided to get a job you probably don't challenge her right to criticize you. Did you ask for her approval? Do you wonder about her motives? No, you assume that this unsolicited criticism is within her right and province as your friend. And on top of all that you feel guilty. Some friend.

Criticism may be motivated by jealousy or resentment on the part of the critic. He may need to keep you down to feel adequate himself. When Jean decided to leave her public relations job to work on a book, she was startled and upset that her boss, who had been supportive in the past, undermined her decision and suggested that she would fail through lack of ability. In fact, the criticism came from the boss's jealousy and not Jean's incompetence. Jean made the common mistake of assuming that her boss knew more than she did. If you believe that everybody knows more than you, it's time to rearrange your thinking process. Some people do—and others don't.

We also assume that our critic has better judgment. Again, this may be true sometimes, but not always. You, not the other person, are the best judge of your behavior and choices. If you accept another's judgment you may be in the same situation that Shelley was in when she began attending Florence's criticism workshop.

Shelley worked as a secretary and dreamed of becoming a writer. She finally signed up for a creative writing course at night at a local college. When she told her boss, he laughed at her decision, suggesting that creative writing was a waste of time, that few writers were ever published, and that the only profit would go to the teacher who was taking her money. The real future, he told her, was in computer courses. Shelley soon switched to computer programming.

She was vaguely depressed and dissatisfied when she came to the workshop. Instead of listening to her boss, whose opinion was influenced by *his* needs, Shelley needed to examine her *own* motives for going to school. Was it to improve her mind or her skills, or both? Was it an extension of her job or not?

In the clinic, Shelley learned to analyze the real issues that were facing her. Her boss's criticism was based on the value he placed on earning money and the sort of worker he needed at the office—but Shelley was making enough money to satisfy her needs in her secretarial job and her priorities were different. Shelley had placed her boss in a fatherly role and felt that she ought to take his advice because he knew best. Once she realized what she had done, she dropped the computer programming course and joined a writers' workshop. And next fall she'll take that creative writing course. Shelley may never sell an article, but at least she has the satisfaction of knowing that she's made her own decision to do what *she* wants to do.

———— • ————

It's important to learn how to recognize different *types* of criticism. Criticism may be *constructive*, or it may have a *hidden agenda;* it may be *constant*, or it may be *subjective.* To deal with a critical comment in a healthy manner you must be able to analyze it.

The Criticism Crumble

Constructive criticism improves you or something you have done. Most often you have asked for it by soliciting the opinion of a person you respect, a person whose judgment you value. If you accept the criticism, you or your work will be improved, and you won't feel stupid or put down because the criticism is given at an intellectual level instead of an emotional one.

The *hidden agenda critic* says one thing and means another. You'll be more effective in dealing with this critic if you try to understand the hidden agenda—after all, you can't solve a problem until you know what it is. Sometimes simply telling a hidden agenda critic that you're able to cope with criticism may help him to be direct with you.

Karen worked for a drug rehabilitation program administered by the state government, and her boss was a hidden agenda critic. Part of the program was funded by a federal grant, and for the administrative purpose of keeping the grant, her boss needed to show statistical evidence that a certain number of men were moving from prison to work release. Instead of explaining his dilemma, he criticized Karen. "You've had enough time to get the men ready. Why aren't more of them in work release?" She knew that you don't effect a psychological cure by a time clock, but her boss's insistence, coupled with his inability to communicate the administrative point of view, led them both to make mistakes.

Sometimes the hidden agenda critic is simply unable to be critical directly. Many wives complain of husbands who belittle the time they spend at evening meetings. They make fun of women's groups and imply that nothing is ever accomplished but gossip. What the hidden agenda husband is unable to say is, "I feel lonely and I miss you when you go out without me at night." The thought underlying his negative comments is a positive one.

Of all the critics, the *constant critic* is the most wearing. He will find fault no matter what you do. He may be acting out of his own insecurity or the mistaken belief that criticism is the only way to keep his employees on their toes. Whatever his reasons, there are techniques for making life with a constant critic bearable.

Try agreeing with him. If you agree long enough, he'll run out of criticism. Or try another ploy. Since the constant critic tends to hand out blanket criticism, force him to be specific about his dislikes. For example, if he says he doesn't like your reports, ask him if he means the style, the content, or the statistical information. And remember to ask him what he *likes* about your performance. After all, he must have some reason for not firing you. You'll find the constant critic often cools his criticism when asked for an honest appraisal of your work.

This technique worked for Julia, an efficient and innovative program director for the local mental health agency. She was thinking of quitting her job because her boss, who was threatened by Julia's obvious ability, was sabotaging her efforts by criticizing her programs, removing her authority, and making her accountable for each and every action. Quitting might have been a good idea had Julia not enjoyed the work she performed in the community. But first she had to be able to make the decision rationally instead of emotionally.

After attending Florence's criticism clinic, Julia stopped reacting emotionally to her boss's constant criticism. She challenged her, requesting specific examples of what was wrong with the programs. As Julia stood up to her, her boss—like most bullies—retreated. After several months, her own incompetence (the reason she had felt threatened in the first place) came to the attention of the board of directors. She was fired, and Julia was given her job.

Subjective criticism may contain one or more elements of truth, but it also includes a value judgment on the part of the critic. Before you respond to this criticism, be careful to separate the valid from the subjective.

The Criticism Crumble

Take the case of a well-known lawyer who's noted for her flamboyant style of dressing. When a friend commented, "Don't you think your orange blouse and purple skirt are inappropriate?" she responded politely, "No. If I did, I wouldn't be wearing them." If the lawyer hadn't thought about the color combination, she might have responded with, "I'll think about it." But she *had* considered the color combination and liked it. Whether or not the colors are inappropriate is a subjective value judgment on the part of her critic. If you've considered what you're doing, never be swayed by the subjective value judgment of another.

Most of us become emotional when we're criticized. We *deny, defend, counterattack,* or *atone.* For example, imagine that your boss comes into the office while you're on the telephone. "Don't you ever do any work?" he accuses.

The *denier* responds, "I'm hardly ever on the phone. I don't know what you mean."

The *defender* says, "I just picked it up this second; it just rang. I didn't know you'd be angry."

The *counterattacker* says, "Well, you're always on the phone when the president calls, and I have to cover for you."

The *atoner* accepts the criticism meekly. "I'm sorry. I'll never do it again. Please excuse me."

None of these responses will help you get ahead or feel good about yourself.

The *denier* is afraid to accept responsibility. Nothing is ever her fault. Such an approach will automatically keep her at a lower-level job because reliability and dependability are vital for success in the business world. Most employers will not chastise the employee who admits and takes responsibility for her mistakes.

Defenders suffer from low self-esteem. Defending and justifying waste psychic energy and don't bring recognition as a promotable employee.

Counterattackers succeed in deflecting criticism away from themselves, but they alienate their coworkers and lose the valuable elements that may be inherent in criticism.

Atoners are the least likely to succeed in any endeavor because they don't have the self-confidence to question. They believe that anybody's judgment is superior to theirs—their critic is always correct.

————— • —————

You're going to be in a better position to deal with criticism when you accept it as a normal part of your daily life. The criticism crumble vanishes the minute you learn to light your way out of the criticism box with the LAMP method: *Listen, Analyze, Make a decision,* and *Practice.*

Listen with your brain instead of your emotions, analyze the critic and the criticism, make a decision on how to deal with the criticism, and practice dealing with criticism in your daily life. Your brain is as sophisticated a computer as any you are using at the office. Use it to process data at an intellectual level.

Composed listening projects power. You can listen to criticism without falling apart or panicking—because listening doesn't mean that you're accepting the criticism as correct. The minute you interrupt your critic to justify, deny, explain, or point out his mistake you're actively involving yourself with the criticism and allowing it to become an emotional issue.

Sometimes listening is painful. In this kind of situation, try the diffusing method of agreeing with your critic but using such qualifying words as "sometimes," "maybe," or "perhaps." These words take the sting out of the criticism and imply that you're not perfect and don't *have* to be perfect.

Check out your critic as you listen to him. Does he deliver criticism emotionally or intellectually? Is he an accurate observer of fact? Is your value system different from his?

Always analyze the criticism and the critic to determine whether you're dealing with constructive, hidden agenda, constant, or subjective criticism. And remember that sometimes the hardest critic to deal with is yourself. Men and women can be sabotaged in their efforts for success by critical messages from their past that have little bearing on present reality.

Dolores is a competent commercial artist. At her drawing board she feels like the talented professional she is, but those good feelings about herself vanish the second she sits at the conference table. She clams up and has difficulty selling her ideas. She feels inadequate and is convinced that everybody else at the meeting is smarter and better qualified than she is.

Dolores is sabotaging herself with feelings left over from her childhood. Seated at the dining room table each night listening to her four talkative brothers argue community problems with her parents, she decided that she was dumb because she had nothing to contribute. It never occurred to her that her lack of knowledge was simply the result of being the youngest of five children. Those negative feelings about herself still surface when she sits at the conference table twenty-five years later.

Like Dolores, many of us continue to think of ourselves in terms of the labels our parents gave us. Mom may have called you the bright one, the creative one, the sloppy one, or the disorganized one. Whatever the label, take time to unstick it before it colors your professional life.

When you have listened and analyzed the criticism, you're ready to make a decision on how to deal with it. Accept it if it's an accurate statement of fact; reject it if it's not. If it's trivial, you can just ignore it. If you're not clear about it, ask questions to be sure you understand it. If you're uncertain about how to answer your critic, try to defer your response. You don't have to give an immediate answer to a critical comment.

You may decide to change some of your habits, but there are others you may decide to keep. For instance, you may work at a messy desk, but know where everything is. It's your active choice not to waste time by organizing your papers into neat little piles. And that's perfectly okay!

Remember too that criticism is sometimes built into the system and has nothing to do with your actual performance. Melissa worked for the city government; she had been praised by her superiors for the job she was doing and felt secure in her performance—until her immediate boss showed her *his* appraisal of her work. He had rated her as good in some instances, but only satisfactory in others. Had she accepted this as an honest evaluation, her self-esteem would have suffered. Instead, she checked her critic out, and discovered that he was required to maintain a medium range in his appraisals. If he had rated her excellent that year, he wouldn't have been able to give her a raise the following year. His criticism was built into the system and had nothing to do with her actual performance.

Some of us are so sensitive to criticism that we need to practice desensitizing ourselves at home. If you fall into this category, make a list of all your faults, even the ones that nobody knows but you. Then go over them, remembering to use qualifying words—"Sometimes I'm disorganized" or "I *tend* to have difficulty dealing with people at work." This won't have the same effect as it would if another person were delivering the criticism, but it will familiarize you with possible criticism.

Many of us find *giving* criticism as difficult as accepting it. When you give criticism to subordinates, remember not to place the blame on anybody. After all, placing blame will not correct the problem. Try not to criticize when you're angry or upset—the chances are that you won't get your facts straight if you're in an excited state.

Criticism is not an opportunity to take revenge. You don't have to be cruel or malicious. Learn to separate the facts (what *is*) from your subjective value system (what you would *like*). Be sure that your facts are correct, then deliver them objectively in a well-modulated tone. Don't start with phrases like "You should have done it this way" or "If only you hadn't done it this way." It *did* happen. That and only that is the issue.

Use this formula when you're giving criticism: state a positive part of the problem, then state the problem, tell how it can be corrected, and, finally, how the correction will solve the problem.

———————•———————

Throughout your life you will criticize and be criticized. Some of that criticism will be fair and some will be unjust, but you won't crumble if you remember to deal with criticism *intellectually* instead of *emotionally*. LISTEN, ANALYZE, MAKE A DECISION, and PRACTICE.

CHAPTER 6

Crisis Thinking

Jeanette holds a sales position with an electronics corporation. Her capabilities suggest that she's a young woman with excellent career potential, but Jeanette may never make it to the top. Why? Because she's a crisis thinker, an employee with an emotional approach to business situations. Her behavior is definitely not what's expected of a professional. For example, when her marketing manager told Jeanette that a small contract had been lost through her mishandling of a customer, she immediately burst into tears. At the outset, Jeanette's boss had planned to go over different sales approaches with her and show her how to mend fences with the client. Instead he was forced to deal with her emotion.

Crisis thinking, an emotional response to an event, is common to women. The crisis thinker is dominated by *feeling* rather than *fact*, she *reacts* rather than *acts*. And since she doesn't weigh alternatives or think situations through to their logical conclusions, the crisis thinker often makes an irrational decision.

If you want to be a winner at work you'll have to cure yourself of crisis thinking. The employee who handles all problems as if they are crises calls the worst kind of attention to herself. "Hassles, not crises form the bulk of our business day," says the personnel director of a major corporation. "Orders are cancelled, employees quit, jobs are over- or underbid, deadlines must be met, and contracts drawn. Many of our women employees are unable to differentiate between various kinds of problems and see everything at the office as having the same level of magnitude. They drain their energy and make poor decisions because of their emotional approach."

By now you may be wondering how you wound up a crisis thinker while the man at the next desk is calm, cool, collected, and professional. It doesn't seem fair. Like many other behavior patterns, crisis thinking comes from early socialization and your lack of familiarity with the office. The man at the next desk has been socialized for the business game since childhood—but what about you?

You were brought up believing that it was acceptable for little girls to cry, that women could be emotional and not bother about analyzing their problems. Boys are taught to solve problems, be logical, and hide their emotions. These differences are reinforced from the time you're an infant. During their first weeks, male babies tend to be more irritable than female babies, so their mothers pick them up and give them more stimulation. On the other hand, girls are more sensitive to touch, cold, pain, and variations in sound. Girls walk earlier, smile more, and utter more sounds; they're docile and receptive to social stimuli, while boys are aggressive.

Many studies have attempted to explore the roots of these behavior patterns. A particularly intriguing one by Michael Lewis showed that mothers tend to hold their sons on their laps facing out into the world which they will later explore and conquer, while little girls are held facing in, safe within the familiar environment of their mother's arms, breast, and face. Mothers toss toys across the room for their sons to retrieve, but they hand toys to their daughters.

A girl's early training leads her away from independent

thinking. While the little boy thinks "What do I want?" the little girl thinks "What do they want of me?" Success is gauged in terms of meeting the demands of others, pleasure comes from pleasing others, and self-esteem is dependent on the feelings of others. On the other hand, the role expectations of "being masculine" include independence, action, aggressiveness, competition, winning, and achieving.

Throughout their lives, boys are rewarded for exploring their environment, even though they tear their pants climbing trees and fall in streams in search of frogs and minnows. Little girls are rewarded for being good, clean, quiet, and well behaved. While little boys were learning to be aggressive, independent, dominant, and competitive—traits that win at work—you were learning to be passive, emotional, loving, and supportive.

Sex-role training for boys is more strenuous in the early years because a boy must shift his early identification with his mother to his father—but from then on he learns his behavior patterns more consistently than a girl does. Both parents put pressure on him to conform to the sex-role stereotype. Being a sissy, crying, retreating when attacked, wearing girls' clothes, or playing with dolls is discouraged. On the other hand, a girl may be a tomboy, wear jeans, and play with trucks and guns—and nobody minds.

Preschool boys tend to be interested in toys and objects, while little girls tend to prefer people. Boys are aggressive on the playground, either initiating or being the target of aggression, while little girls cluster in groups, submit or argue, but rarely fight.

A boy's early training at home and school is expanded when he takes part in sports and in the armed forces. According to Betty Harragan, author of *Games Your Mother Never Taught You,* the rules of business are reenforced through both these experiences. The military is organized in a chain of command similar to the one at the office; activities on the playing fields train young men in teamwork and winning. Often this includes using a devious approach—faking, stealing, and subterfuge are all accepted modes of behavior on the football and baseball field, and in many businesses too. Obviously, these sports ethics are quite different from the ethics of the home which women bring to the office.

In her clinical experience, Florence has found that the journey from home to office is easier for women who have shared a close friendship with their fathers. This stems from the fact that fathers play a more important part in sex-role stereotyping than mothers do. In many cases, a father provides his daughter with an effective management model, and company interviewers often consider the impact of a father's relationship a crucial factor in gauging a young woman's business potential.

A district plant supervisor with the telephone company sees her close relationship with her father as the main reason for her success in business. "We were a family of girls, so my father picked me to be his 'son.' I learned to hunt and fish and enjoyed the time he spent telling me about his export business. He used to take me on business trips, and I think I absorbed many of his thinking patterns."

An electronics engineer recalls that her father never differentiated between the girls and boys in the family. "He said that the same doors were there for all of us. All we had to do was push them open and walk through. We could be anything we chose as long as we were willing to work for it."

Many years ago, when a woman who later became a judge was turned down by several law schools because of her sex, it was her father's constant encouragement that softened the blow and gave her the confidence to apply elsewhere. "In order to succeed," she says, "a woman needs the love and support of one decent man in her life—preferably her father."

Many women don't get that kind of support from their fathers. In fact, a father may denigrate women who want to work and encourage his daughter to stay at home like a "real woman." "My father always made fun of my advanced degrees," says a woman who is now a clinical psychologist. "When I opened a clinical testing service he joked about it with his friends. He used to say 'I don't know why any thinking person would go to Alice for help, when she couldn't help herself by staying home and getting married." Alice acknowledges that pursuing her career might have been easier if she had not been criticized by her father. Another young woman who attended one of Florence's workshops commented that her father thought it was a fine idea for her to work "as long as my job doesn't threaten my husband."

———————•—•———————

Parents and society still sanction the stereotype of the feeling woman and the thinking man. Unfortunately, when that feeling woman goes to work, she falls into the clutch of crisis thinking. She perceives a whole variety of issues as life-and-death situations that need rapid solutions.

Crisis thinkers get caught in a number of different traps. For example, they often tend to take the recommendations of the staff member who talks the loudest and the most persuasively instead of the one with the best advice. Loudness may project strength when you're feeling weak, but the person who talks the loudest may not be the best qualified to give you good information. In fact, if a person's voice is raised he may be upset himself or using the technique to intimidate others.

The person with the best advice may often be the one who's quiet and logical, not the one who's loud. If you're often under control and not vulnerable yourself, you'll be able to test the shouter by raising *your* voice or confronting him directly to see if he backs down.

When your emotions are in charge, you're apt to be swayed by the person who reacts the same way you do and accepts your sense of urgency. This person may also be using the "mirror" technique to gain more acceptance from you. By "mirroring" your behavior—nodding, say, when you do, or leaning forward when you do—the person forges an unconscious bond between you.

Crisis thinkers tend to tap their emotion by complaining about job injustices to people, either at home or on the job, who can't do anything to help the situation. Jennie, an administrative assistant in an insurance office, felt as if she were stuck in her job. By the time she'd trained her third supervisor, she was beginning to wonder why *she* didn't have the job. She complained about the injustice to her friends and to her family, but she didn't take her complaint to the company. The bad job was more comfortable than the risk, effort, and energy that might be involved in a complaint—especially because she would have to go over the new supervisor's head. Jennie never did anything to correct her situation.

If you're like Jennie, complaining about your job may seem safer than looking for a new one. It also has one big advantage. People will listen to your miserable story of being ripped off—at least for awhile. The attention that you get from your audience can even become a positive part of the job. If you quit, you'll lose that—and so the cycle continues.

Many adult relationships are based on the unwritten contract that if one person is miserable the other will try to make him feel better. But sometimes this can backfire when frustration sets in and the person playing nurse realizes that there isn't going to be a cure.

If you find that you're spending a lot of time complaining about your job, ask yourself a few questions. What am I getting out of complaining? Is complaining meeting an unfulfilled emotional need? Why have I chosen not to complain to anybody who could make a constructive change in my situation? Am I afraid of losing my job or am I afraid of losing the compassionate listeners who make me the center of attention? If you need to complain to be noticed and to feel important you should reexamine your lifestyle. You'll discover that you can have more rewarding relationships in sharing a common interest or hobby than in sharing complaints about your job, your spouse, or your mother-in-law.

———————————

Don't be surprised if you're a crisis thinker at work and calm, cool, and collected at home. Unlike the office, home is your turf—you've been socialized to belong there. Familiarity with your turf allows you to differentiate between a problem and a real crisis.

Sharon attended Florence's workshop because crisis thinking was hampering her progress at work. She saw every delay, order change, or client disagreement in her architectural office as a crisis. "I could understand it if I were overwrought and emotional at home, but I'm not. I handle emergencies with the house and the kids every day." She told the group a dramatic story that serves as an illustration of the crisis thinker who can be calm and competent at home.

A neighbor's child developed a severe allergy reaction while playing at Sharon's house. As soon as the child began gasping for breath Sharon called the doctor. Realizing that this was an acute emergency, the doctor told her how to perform an emergency tracheotomy in case she didn't reach the hospital in time. Calmly, Sharon sterilized a knife and placed it and the child in her car. Luckily, she arrived at the hospital in time.

Sharon couldn't understand why she was able to deal with a child who was choking to death and yet was unable to remain calm when shingles for her client's roof didn't arrive on schedule. In the workshop Sharon learned to loosen the crisis clutch by adopting a creative, adult thinking plan. In creative adult thinking, your brain becomes the administrator of your emotions. You are in charge of yourself and others. This logical, intellectual approach involves *sizing up a situation* before making a decision, and *suiting your behavior* to fit the situation. Here's an example.

Peggy, the section head at a restaurant, asks the busboy to clean off a table. He ignores her and goes to the kitchen. The restaurant is busy. The *facts* of the problem are that Peggy is the supervisor and is responsible for making sure the tables are clean. The busboy is paid to clear the tables; he is responsible to her. Her *options* are to clear the table herself, leave it, or find another way to make him do the job. If she clears the tables herself, she will always be doing it; if she ignores the mess, she may lose her job. Instead she takes the busboy aside, looks him in the eye, and firmly tells him that he'll be fired if he doesn't clear the table. This kind of decision is especially difficult for many women because they have difficulty being assertive when subordinates refuse to do their jobs. But Peggy had considered her options and knew that this course was the only constructive one.

Creative, adult thinking works in all kinds of situations— those that require a quick decision, like Peggy's, and those that take some time to develop, like Paula's.

Paula was an office manager-secretary for a company selling business equipment. Several new salesmen were added to the sales force, and Paula discovered that she had more work than she could handle—especially since much of her typing had to be done on a deadline. This happened despite her boss's promise that she would have a minimum of extra work.

Here's how a creative adult thinking plan worked in Paula's situation. The *problem* is between Paula and her boss. The *facts* of the problem are that Paula's workload has increased and she can't get it done on deadline without working late. Her *options* include quitting, staying late to complete her assignments, asking for a raise to make her additional work worthwhile, and asking for a typist. Since Paula cannot afford to be unemployed, even for a few weeks, she could also look for another job before she talks to her boss. And what are the consequences of all these options? If she works late, Paula will have less time to herself and not be paid for time that she's giving the firm. If she talks to her boss, she may be given a raise or help with the typing; but if her boss refuses to do anything, she'll have to look for a new job.

Paula thought her problem through, and remembering her boss's unfulfilled promises, decided to look for another job before she talked to him. Although this took an extra effort, she was in a much stronger position when they discussed the problem. Her job hunting had given her an extra feeling of security, so that when she finally confronted her boss she was able to deal calmly with the situation—and successfully lobby for both a raise and extra help.

Remember that you won't get fired just for talking. No reasonable boss will dismiss you for presenting your thoughts and feelings in a logical manner. Talk is simply an exchange of information; often it's a valuable way to clear the air. Unfortunately, little girls who have been programmed to be seen and not heard are fearful of taking the initiative in exploring a job problem with their boss. "I've been programmed since birth for a man to take the lead. I wait for his initiative and I expect him to *know* that I'm dissatisfied without my saying anything," explains an executive secretary. She feels this way about both her boss *and* her husband.

———————

After you've had a chance to practice the technique of creative adult thinking you'll soon be making rapid decisions without needing to remind yourself of the points on the following checklist. Until then, remember these steps:

Use your brain power. Size up a situation before you act and ask appropriate questions. Keep your emotions under control while you focus on a problem and get the facts. When the brain is in control, you remain free from guilt over what you should have done and free from fear over what may happen to you. For example, Beth's assistant presented her with a crisis when she announced that the quarterly report for the federal grant money to fund their women's center was not complete. When you're presented with another person's interpretation of a crisis you need to use your mind, not your emotions. Beth kept calm, asked for the government grant regulations on dates for applying for funding, and then checked through the original documents and grant materials and asked for an exact account on the state of the report. When she discovered that the report *was* due and that it *was* nowhere near completion, she realized that this was not the time to ask her staff for lengthy explanations. Instead, she called the federal agency and requested an extension on the project, and after it was granted she sent out a confirming letter to the agency and an explanatory letter to her board. She thought her crisis through to its logical conclusion because she didn't panic.

Suit your behavior to your goal. Calculate whether a mild, moderate, or strong approach will be the most effective in your particular situation. A mild approach is a questioning one—low-keyed, docile, and retiring. A moderate approach uses a firm, well-modulated tone to make a statement. A strong approach can be as forceful as the situation warrants—as long as you remain in control of that force.

Each approach is effective in different situations. A strong approach may be necessary in a situation in which, say, you've been promised a raise and still haven't received it. On the other hand, if you're dealing with a rigid, authoritarian boss, you may choose a mild approach.

Remember the ground rules. The seventies have become the female twilight zone. Old stereotypes are breaking down, and women are discovering more options at work than they ever had before, but many women are going off half cocked because they're unfamiliar with business rules. Remember these ten DONT'S at the office:

1. *Don't cry.* Tears confirm the male stereotype of an emotional woman; crying can often be emotional blackmail. Laurie was an engineer for a major corporation who made the mistake of crying in a meeting with her manager. As a result, he decided that although she was an excellent engineer and adept at solving complex energy problems he would not be able to send her out on the road to meet with clients because her emotion would jeopardize job consultations.

2. *Don't whine.* Whining is childlike and offensive to the ear. Remember that there's a correlation between the way you sound and the way people think of you. Practice listening to yourself.

Margot, a newspaper reporter, adopted a little girl whine when she spoke to her boss about several new assignments. Her boss whined right back at her, and after a moment of stunned silence Margot burst out laughing. Until that moment she hadn't realized how offensive she sounded.

3. *Don't model yourself after a man in your dress or demeanor*—you'll only become a pseudowoman who's going nowhere. An aggressively pushy woman will turn a man off. The best advice is to think like a man, but always look and behave like *yourself*.

4. *Discuss, but don't argue.* You'll lose office power if you indulge in a long and heated argument—and if your boss doesn't agree with you, you may be considered disruptive. Present all the facts you can to back up your case, but avoid long, circular arguments. Accept the fact that your boss has the right to the final decision. Recognize the moment when you have lost your

point and back off gracefully.

5. *Don't talk negatively about your boss or your company to anybody inside the company.* The office grapevine will guarantee that all negative comments will boomerang back to your boss. If he hears that you think he's a rat he may think twice about promoting you—or he may promote you into a different and less rewarding area to get you out of his hair. Most companies demand loyalty from their employees, and it's poor policy to bite the hand that's feeding you. There's always somebody else to fill your job, and she may get it if you aren't careful with your tongue.

6. *Don't take the kids to work.* This may seem obvious to career women, but the part-time worker or mother returning to the work force has to remember to keep her home and job separate. The best-behaved child is not an asset at the office. You'll be labelled unprofessional by your associates, and your kids may be used against you at a later date in office politics.

7. *Don't berate your employees in public.* Treat others with respect, no matter what their position. Sometimes the new woman manager who still feels insecure with her position and authority tries to look secure by reprimanding a secretary or a typist in front of the rest of the office. Companies look for good manners in all of their employees. Always call another employee into a private area to discuss a problem and keep the discussion on the problem and not the person. The issue is not whether or not the other person is dumb or irresponsible, but how an error can be corrected.

8. *Don't get involved in romantic relationships at work.* Romantic attachments aren't going to help you get ahead at work. In fact, they may hold you back; the bedroom is *not* the way to the boardroom. Once an affair is over, you may find that you're vulnerable and expendable; the man may not want to have you around to reveal his secrets. Unfortunately, the old rule still seems to apply—it's okay for men to have office af-

fairs, but not for women. The woman who does indulge in affairs becomes the subject of office gossip and loses her image of professionalism.

9. *Don't talk about your health.* Your personal physiology is not part of your office life. Take care of it on your own, and if you must talk about it, unburden yourself to friends outside the office.

10. *Don't be a troublemaker.* Not getting along with others is a corporate sin. And here's one area where you can finally use all those years of early training in which you were taught to put people at ease. Don't sell those female skills of sympathy, warmth, and understanding short. They may be more valuable than you think. A recent survey in a sales management magazine stated that clients prefer salesmen who don't look or act like salesmen. What better salesperson than a woman who can put her client at ease first and then deliver her pitch? It may take a man years to learn what many women have been socialized to do naturally.

Keep a creative adult thinking log. Keeping your own log for a week will give you a valuable office profile. Start by logging in the problem. Just writing it down will help to clarify it in your own mind. Then write down the players (who's involved), followed by the facts concerning the problem, your different options, and the consequences for each option. Finally, write down your decision. After a week of keeping the log, ask yourself these questions: What kind of problems do I have? Are they more apt to deal with people or procedures? Am I in conflict with one particular person more than others? What qualities do I seem to dislike about him or her? Do I solve problems by delegating authority, or do I feel that I have to do everything myself?

Crisis Thinking

Strange as it may seem, you may actually reach the point where you can make a crisis work *for* you. A crisis may be sought out instead of dreaded. Well handled and solved, it calls attention to your management capabilities. In fact, many successful businessmen use the technique of *creating* a crisis for the sole purpose of solving it. "You don't get noticed sitting in your office quietly getting things done," explained one executive.

If an office problem comes up, you have the option of magnifying it by choice so that you can solve it and gain attention. Solving a crisis may make you feel better about yourself since your self-esteem evolves through setting goals and attaining them. Those goals may be simple ones like getting the office paperwork out on time or major ones like getting a contract, but the inner dynamics remain the same.

Whether you're in the first stages of battling crisis thinking, or moving up to become a crisis-monger, it helps to keep your perspective—and your sense of humor. Remember the story of the business executive who holds his mail unopened for a week. His premise, which is definitely not that of a crisis thinker, is that half of the problems in the mail will have gone away by the end of the week. The other half he'll solve.

CHAPTER 7

Anger Is Good For You

———————◆—————————

Amy is ready to go home when her boss hands her a report which must be typed by nine A.M. She has been looking forward to seeing her son pitch for his Little League team, but she smiles brightly at her boss and says that she doesn't mind working late. Amy arrives home three hours later with a migraine headache and yells at her son for leaving his baseball bat in the front hall. Her suppressed anger at her boss has surfaced in both her migraine and the scene with her son.

Suppressed anger may be channeled in a variety of unexpected ways. Recent research has suggested that cancer, ulcers, high blood pressure, colitis, migraine headaches, and depression can all be connected with unexpressed anger. There is a crucial relationship between the ability to feel and release anger and one's sense of emotional and physical well-being. The emotionally healthy adult knows how to release her anger at a primitive level and how to deliver it at a social level.

———————◆—————————

There's nothing wrong with anger. In fact, men and women can use the energy created by anger to do things that might be impossible under normal circumstances. During the Second World War, an associate of Florence's discovered that anger

106

was a therapeutic tool for combatting the severe depression suffered by paraplegic veterans. These men were sunk in such severe depression that they refused to have any contact with the world around them—but when the doctor placed them on a ward with a verbally abusive nurse she made them so angry that they had to get well to retaliate. Divorce lawyers are also familiar with the energy produced by anger. It often helps to carry their clients through the traumatic stages of divorce proceedings.

Unfortunately, many of us are not able to express anger, and suppressing that anger is what gets us into trouble. A teenager who is angry at her parents runs away instead of confronting the situation; a wife denies her anger at her husband and wonders why she experiences sexual dysfunction; a woman who is angry about her job suffers from sick headaches. All of these people are suppressing their anger—and suppressed anger can sometimes have disastrous consequences. Florence's observations of inmates at a state prison show that most murderers who had killed for the first time were quiet, timid people. If they had been able to express their anger, their acts of violence might have been prevented.

Until quite recently, expressing anger was taboo in our society. Being "in control" was the mark of good breeding and social class. Since society didn't provide an acceptable outlet for anger, men and women either suppressed it or released it vicariously (and unsatisfactorily) by watching violence on television, attending aggressive sporting events, and reading each and every gory detail about a murder.

You have been trained to be afraid of your own anger and uncomfortable around another person's angry outburst. At almost every step of your development, the socialization process has inhibited your aggressive thinking and behavior. Just think back a minute. Your mother punished you for hitting your little brother. She told you not to talk back or raise your voice. You may have heard such threats as, "If you keep on yelling I'll leave the house and I won't come back," or "When Mommy's dead you'll be sorry you talked like that." The normal expression of anger was gradually inhibited by fear. You learned to suppress your angry feelings because you believed that they might result in abandonment or even death. Inevitably this kind of training produces an adult who is unable to express or deal with anger.

Some people suppress their anger because they equate the loss of control with weakness. They believe that their ironclad discipline gives them a permanent posture of authority—when all it really does is make them seem cold and rigid. What they don't realize is that people are more likely to relate to them in a human, caring way when they expose the real person instead of a phony facade.

When anger is released it will run its brief course. When anger is suppressed it leads to depression, is channeled into indirect expressions, or explodes into violence. A violent expression of anger doesn't have to be physical—the verbally violent person will assault you with insulting and obnoxious behavior.

Often inanimate objects such as the government, the potholes in the road, or the state of the world masquerade as objects of your anger simply because they're safe. The husband who indulges in tirades about the income tax may actually be telling his wife, "I'm angry with you because you're spending more money than I can afford, but I don't know how to tell you."

———————

You'll find that your performance and your health will suffer if you're unable to release your anger—it takes a lot of energy to keep that anger at a level that won't be visible to yourself or others. Women who attend Florence's workshops are often surprised by the physical changes they feel when they learn to get their anger out.

When Lisa attended the first session of an anger assessment workshop she claimed that she never got angry—but ever since she had changed jobs several months earlier she had had an incipient ulcer. Lisa worked for a small engineering firm in a secretarial capacity. Every Friday her boss prepared the checks for the other employees, and every Friday he overlooked hers. At four o'clock she would knock on his door and ask for her check. At first she told the group that there wasn't any point in "making a big deal" over it, since she always got paid. But later on, when she participated in a role play about the same situation, the truth surfaced—along with Lisa's pent-up anger. "I dread Fridays," she told the workshop member playing her boss. "I feel as if I'm begging from you the way I had to beg from my father for my allowance. I've done my work, and I want to be dignified by a prepared paycheck like everybody else in this office. My secretarial contribution is just as valuable as another employee's engineering." Acting out the situation got Lisa in touch with her suppressed angry feelings and enabled her to confront her boss the following week. Her stomach problems soon disappeared.

Like Lisa, you may have been programmed since birth to believe that it isn't ladylike to get angry. Anger just isn't part of the femininity package for little girls, who are supposed to be made of "sugar and spice and everything nice." When a woman experiences that uncomfortable emotion she tends to suppress it instead of accepting it and learning to deal with it.

There are very few assertive women to serve as role models. Hollywood glorifies the strong, angry man who uses assertive body language and harsh words, but the angry woman (unless, of course, she's protecting her home or children) is called castrating, bitchy, nagging, or masculine. Instead of being encouraged to express anger, women have been urged to take on the role of peacemaker, to become the intermediary who soothes the feelings of others at the expense of her own.

But those feelings don't go away, no matter how much you'd like them to. Instead, they may only be camouflaged by depression or other indirect expressions of anger. Depression is unexpressed anger, anger that has been turned in on yourself instead of out against another person—where it belongs. Suicide is the ultimate form of anger against oneself, even though many suicidal people believe that they will punish somebody else by killing themselves.

Depression often originates in the anger that comes from being in a dependent situation, when a person feels, "I can't do it myself. I need you to do it for me." Marriage by itself does not create dependencies, but when already dependent people marry they can become trapped in the kind of relationship that leads to anger.

Florence has found that depression is a socially acceptable way for women to cope with anger because "moodiness" may be associated with the female menstrual cycle. Society allows you your depression, but let's face it—it isn't any fun.

One of the first signs of depression is constant fatigue. Many women are chronically tired no matter how much sleep they get. This fatigue disguises their anger and resentment over any number of problems they might have. Their energy level increases dramatically when they get out of their rut and begin to participate in activities that they enjoy. An hour or two a week may be all you need to jolt you out of a depression. Just look at the thousands of sweet, accommodating women who put on their short, white dresses several days a week and smash a tennis ball across a net.

Physical activity is one of the best ways to release angry feelings, and if you don't believe it watch the expressions on those tennis players as they serve and stroke the ball! "I believed that I should help my kids and husband instead of blowing up at them," says the charming wife of a prominent banker. "But when I played tennis I pretended that little white ball was the son who never cleaned up his room, or the daughter who wasn't speaking to me, or the husband who was late for dinner. For one hour I slammed my family all over the court and felt marvelous about it. The angrier I was, the better my game."

The chronic fatigue that goes hand in hand with depression often makes women believe that they have an undiagnosed illness. Madge was working as a telephone operator to put her husband through college. The pay was good, and Madge did her job well, but she was always tired. When she consulted her doctor, she was surprised to learn that she was in excellent health. He asked if there were any emotional problems or conflicts in her life. Was she happy in her marriage? Did she like her job?

The more Madge thought about her job, the more she realized that she hated it. She was a big, strong woman who had grown up on a farm and loved the outdoors. "Every time I walk through the company's front door I feel as if I'm going to prison," she said. Once Madge accepted the fact that she was angry with her job and angry about being the sole family support, she stopped brooding about having an incurable illness and was able to take steps to change her situation. Luckily for her, her dissatisfaction with her job came at a time when the company had opened up a program of nontraditional jobs for women. Today she works as a lineman and wakes each morning feeling enthusiastic and invigorated. Not every woman wants to wear heavy boots and a twenty-pound belt around her waist, and not every woman wants to set and climb telephone poles, but Madge loves the freedom of being outside instead of being cooped up in an office.

One of the hallmarks of depression is the feeling that your situation is hopeless, that *you* are hopeless. In some cases, the problem that's causing the depression is so deeply buried that you're left with a vague feeling of distress—you literally "don't know what's the matter with you." Sometimes this feeling is relieved simply by discovering and accepting the cause of your depression, even though you may not be able to change it. For example, since they depended on her income, Madge might have had to stay with a job she didn't like until her husband was through college. In this case, she could have accepted her anger over being indoors, agreed with her husband that she was going to quit the minute he was through school, and immediately taken up a hobby like backpacking or jogging or bicycling that met her need to be outside.

Some women who must work in boring jobs while their husbands are completing college keep large calendars to mark off the days. "Every day that I make a large, red X on my calendar I feel a little better," says a woman who is putting her husband through law school. On really bad days, she scribbles out the whole square in red pencil—and scribbles some of her anger out too.

The most common behavior patterns associated with indirect anger are *sabotage, physical illness,* and *displacement.*

There are many different ways to *sabotage* the person with whom you're angry. If you're angry with your boss for giving your additional work, you may use your office flex time to schedule a doctor's appointment on the morning when you know there's an important meeting. If you're angry with your husband you may leave his suit at the cleaners on the day before he plans to leave town on a business trip. In both cases, you become so sorry and apologetic that the sabotaged boss or husband has to comfort you. It's a tricky little maneuver. You're either denying or are not even aware of your own angry feelings, and you're making the other person feel guilty, all at the same time.

Forgetting is the most common form of sabotage. If you're constantly forgetful, it's most likely that you're not senile or stupid, just angry! Martha worked as a secretary while her husband taught school. Quite often he would ask her to type reports for him at night. Martha smiled sweetly, said yes, and promptly "forgot." Martha was angry that her husband was asking her to continue her secretarial duties at home. She didn't want to look at a typewriter after five o'clock, but she had been brought up to be a good wife who helped her husband. She said "yes" because she felt she ought to—and she forgot because she was angry that her husband had been insensitive to her feelings. When her husband got angry and called her unreliable and undependable, she was punished for not doing what she ought to have done.

It sounds complicated, doesn't it? And that's exactly the kind of round-about game you play when you're not honest with your feelings. Martha would have been happier if she had told her husband straight out that she didn't want to type letters and reports in the evening. She might have told him, "I know you're in a jam, and I don't mind helping occasionally, but I get angry when you don't appreciate my need for some time away from work."

If you're a chronic forgetter, try asking yourself a few simple questions: Do you want to do what you've been asked to do? Do you want to say no, but feel unable to? When you start forgetting to do some important things for yourself—not having your resumes printed up in time for a series of job interviews or having to cancel an appointment because earlier arrangements slipped your mind—your anger is becoming self-destructive.

Being late is another form of sabotage. Traditionally, women kept their men waiting before they finally made their grand entrance. But the office is not the drawing room; it's punctuality that counts. If you're chronically late, check out these questions. Are you angry with the person you're meeting but unable to tell him so? If you're late for an engagement, do you really want to participate in it? If you're late for a meeting, do you feel that your ideas are important to the group? Are you *always* late for engagements with any specific person in your life?

Betty's husband always kept her waiting. "I thought that he didn't have any sense of time so I bought him a watch with an alarm because I felt so rejected sitting alone cooling my heels in restaurants, bars, offices, and railroad stations. But he *still* kept me waiting." Through marriage counseling, Betty and her husband discovered that his lateness stemmed from his anger that Betty was a fulfilled career woman instead of a dependent housewife, which was what he unconsciously wanted his wife to be.

Physical illness is another indirect expression of anger. Have you known somebody who appears to develop a headache the minute she's challenged? That headache is an effective device which not only protects her from her own anger but also from the anger of the other person, who winds up feeling guilty because he caused her headache.

Illness is a cop-out, but it's also painful. Those aches and pains feel *very* real. Wouldn't you prefer to be full of vigor and life instead of being the victim of physical sensations that are the result of unexpressed anger? Get honest with yourself and others, and watch those headaches and stomachaches disappear.

Displacement is a form of indirect anger in which your angry feelings are turned on an innocent party, usually a subordinate. Darlene is the only woman manager in a small but rapidly growing electronics company. The male managers resent her and tend to belittle and joke about her contributions. Instead of standing up to them in an honest confrontation, Darlene picks on her secretary. She has had five secretaries in two years. And while this is obviously hard on secretaries, it's hard on Darlene too because she must sacrifice time from her own job to train each new secretary.

Children are also the victims of displaced office anger since the displacer always shifts his anger to a weaker person whose ability to retaliate will be minimal. Darlene can always find another secretary, and you can always find a reason to yell at your children.

————————

You're going to be more comfortable with yourself and with others when you explode the anger myths in your life and become an anger detective by sleuthing on yourself. Do you con your anger out of the way by being overly sweet, good, and kind when you feel the opposite? Maybe you can identify with Nancy, who cooked her husband a roast beef and Yorkshire pudding dinner the night after he forgot to keep their lunch date. Wouldn't he have been startled to know that she had fixed such a good dinner because she felt like killing him?

Do you hide your feelings behind tears? Tears are one of the few effective physical releases for anger that society allows a woman. A corporate executive tells of a confrontation with a man over an office procedure. "He kept telling me that I was acting as part of a block in the office and not independently—and I knew that wasn't true. When he refused to believe me, I got so angry that I could think of only two things to do—punch him or cry. I chose tears because they seemed more acceptable for a woman, but it would have *felt* better to punch him in the nose."

This woman knew what she was feeling, but many other women who cry are unaware that their *real* emotion is rage. For example, a husband comes home and storms at his wife. The house is a mess; what's she been doing all day, watching TV? She bursts into tears. She knows that she's spent the entire day chasing her toddlers around the house, picking up after them, feeding them, doing the laundry, and giving baths. She hasn't sat down once. She knows all that, but she *doesn't* know that her *real* feeling is fury and frustration at her husband's inability to realize how hard she works.

Some women are so uncomfortable with expressions of their own anger that they try to deny it by smiling or giggling when they make an angry comment. The result, of course, is that they aren't taken seriously.

You may be angry at a coworker who never completes her part of a joint job on schedule. Do you level with her directly? Do you stand up straight, look her in the eye, and say, "I'm angry when I have to cover for you at meetings"? Probably not. Women are more apt to say the same words with a big smile or a deprecating laugh, as if they really don't mean it. If you want to be taken seriously, you must believe in your *right* to be angry.

Are you suppressing or denying angry feelings? One clue is to check out your vocabulary. Florence's clinical experience with women has revealed that many of the sweetest and quietest ladies lace their vocabulary with chilling violence. They smile benignly and say, "I could kill him," "I could strangle him," "I could hang him by his thumbs." June is a classic example of the woman who insists that she never gets angry. Yet in the space of fifteen minutes she told a workshop group that she could kill her husband for being late for dinner, that she would like to murder her children for being late for the bus, and that she often wanted to "knock her two boss's heads together." It's likely that the people who live with June are more in touch with June's angry feelings than she is herself. Start listening to yourself talk. Are you as nonviolent as you think?

———————•—•———————

If you're still uncomfortable about expressing your angry

feelings, you probably have some misconceptions about them. Let's explode a few anger myths.

Getting angry doesn't do you or anyone else any good. Nonsense. In a healthy relationship, both partners must learn to express their anger openly and directly so that it isn't built up and then redirected into a million minor, irrational, and possibly explosive situations. Since you're less apt to express anger to people who are emotionally distant, learning certain techniques to break down the barriers will help improve your communications with the important people in your life. Knowing that your partner is angry and why will strengthen your relationship and tell you more about him. The only waste comes from not working out the anger that's in your relationship.

If I get angry, something terrible might happen. Relax. You don't have that kind of power, and other people are seldom as fragile as you think. If you protect another person by holding back the truth you'll contribute to his immaturity and diminish his self-esteem. Subconsciously, if not consciously, he'll suspect that you think he's unable to handle the situation. Tell him that you're angry and let him make his own conclusions.

Nowhere is the "he can't handle it" syndrome more prevalent than in the case of an alcoholic coworker. Sally's colleague missed a lot of time because of her drinking problem, but the other women at the office—and particularly Sally—felt sorry for the woman. They knew that her marriage was in trouble and that she needed to work, so they excused her drinking, covered up for her, and often did her assignments. They were doing all the wrong things. By protecting her, they were actually encouraging her alcoholism.

Sally was unable to release her own angry feelings about the situation until she attended a workshop. There she practiced saying to her friend, "I know you have a drinking problem and I'm sorry you have many personal problems too, but I'm still

117

angry at having to do your work for you. I'm not going to do it any more. I'm not going to cover for you again."

Sally's friend may not be friendly for a while, but it's better for Sally to put her case on the line honestly and directly. If she refuses to cover up for her friend, she's no longer participating in the woman's destruction. Remember that when you become angry at a person or a situation and honestly air your feelings you're taking care of your primary responsibility—looking out for yourself. And it helps the relationship because you aren't suppressing your feelings. It's a fringe benefit if the other person takes any concrete action because of his confrontation with you.

———— •—— ————

Your anger *belongs* to you and may be used as an available and potent resource as long as you don't hide it, or become afraid of it, or believe that people will think less of you for admitting that you aren't Pollyanna. People who respond negatively to your honest expressions of your feelings aren't constructive participants in your life.

When you discharge your anger assertively, you *approve it, identify the source,* and *confront the problem directly.*

Approve your anger. By now you know that some of us are so adept at hiding our anger that we deny its existence. It may help to remind yourself that you have as many angry feelings as loving ones. If you allow yourself to believe that anger is an important part of you, you'll begin to let it flow into your consciousness. But it's important to remember that feeling anger in all of its intensity doesn't mean you should always *act* on it.

Anger is divided into two categories, the primitive and the social. In many cases, you'll need to release the primitive stage of anger by yelling in the shower, punching a pillow, or whatever else helps you, before dealing with the social stage in which you tell your feelings to another person.

When Susan attended Florence's anger workshop she complained of a depression so severe that any but the most routine household chores were impossible. Susan had suspected for a long time that her husband was having an affair, although she hadn't any proof. Suppressing her anger over his infidelity took so much effort that Susan appeared to be *without* emotion; she spoke in a whispery monotone. Susan seemed like a different woman when she arrived for the last workshop session brimming with energy. What had caused the transformation?

Susan had driven to a market where she rarely shopped and while her car was stopped at a red light she had seen her husband on the sidewalk—with his arm around a girl. "The light was red, so I had to look at them. The windows were closed, but if they'd been open he would have heard me call him every foul word in the English language. I felt a boiling warmth in my chest that I'd never experienced before. It rushed through me and heated my whole body. I could have turned the steering wheel and run over them both, but I didn't. The light changed and I drove home, but that night I confronted my husband and told him to leave."

Susan's suppressed anger had surfaced in all of its intensity, and instead of pushing it down again she had dealt with it—first at a primitive level and later at a social one. She also discovered that she could feel mad enough to kill her husband, but not act it out.

Identify the source of your anger. In the beginning, it may be difficult to learn to release your anger at the appropriate person. Use the same techniques we discussed in tracing the origin of your fears. When an uncomfortable feeling develops—a headache, a knot in your stomach, a crick in your neck, a vague feeling of depression or being "out of sorts"—stop what you're doing and concentrate on the feeling instead of trying to make it go away. Start asking questions. What happened right before your experienced the feeling? Who were you involved with? As you get to the source of each minor irritation you'll become aware of your vulnerabilities.

Edna, a workshop participant, told of receiving a telephone call from her ex-husband. "All of a sudden he wanted me to keep the boys for the weekend, even though he had planned to take them fishing and I had made other plans. I said 'sure' because we had had a bitter custody battle over visitation rights. But when I was driving to work I kept yelling at other motorists, which I never do." She had been afraid to release her anger at her ex-husband, so she vented it on other drivers.

Decide on the timing to release your anger. Deliver your anger as close as possible to the time when it occurs. If you wait, the anger will be diluted and the issues will become cloudy. For example, Edna could have told her husband, "I have plans for the weekend, and I'm angry when you call me at the last minute to make a change. I'll rearrange my schedule for this weekend, but I want you to take the children next weekend." That way she could have released her anger and allowed it to run its course. By keeping it in, she displaces it on innocent bystanders. She also begins to brood about the custody battle. "If I were a good mother, I'd want these kids all the time, especially after I fought so hard to get them." Nagging, irrelevant questions like this get in her way.

Whenever possible, deal with irritations as they occur. Sometimes a simple oversight becomes magnified if you don't get the feeling out. Sheila worked for a public relations firm that regularly received free tickets for events in the city. When her boss was sent free tickets for a gala opening of an art exhibit, she told Sheila, "I figured you wouldn't want to go because you go to your mother's on Friday nights, so I gave the tickets to my friend." Sheila felt angry, thought a minute, and then responded. "When you try to read my mind it makes me angry. In this case I *did* want to go to the show because I handled a lot of the publicity for it." There weren't any hard feelings, and Sheila's boss arranged to get two more tickets.

Debbie used a similar technique. She worked for an insurance company, and although her office was small it had a window. When the company moved, Debbie was given a larger office that didn't have a window. Debbie felt angrier and angrier each morning as she walked past the six offices that had windows, particularly since one of the occupants travelled a great deal. The window issue loomed larger and larger in her mind, so she spoke to her boss about it. "I'm angry that I lost my window in the move and that an office with a window was given to a man who's rarely in it." Her boss sympathized with her feelings, and explained that since there were only a few windows the company had decided to give offices with windows on the basis of seniority. Debbie would be next in line for a window office. Debbie didn't get her window right away, but she discovered that airing her feelings changed her whole approach to her own office. She hung pictures on the wall and was content to wait for the day she would get an óffice with a window.

Tell the other person that you're angry. When you're ready to take care of the social aspect of your anger remember that it's the person's *action* not the person himself that has aroused your angry response. Practice delivering your anger by repeating a formula: "I was angry when you...." For example, if a co-worker is habitually late for meetings you might say, "I'm angry when you're late for meetings. We're wasting important time waiting, so from now on we'll have to start without you." Always tell the other person what you've chosen to do to handle a situation that makes you angry.

In an impersonal atmosphere—particularly at work—you'll need to deal with anger by maintaining an intellectual posture instead of an emotional one. If your boss accuses you of something that was not your fault, don't be tempted to get into a "yes, you did; no I didn't" type of argument. Stick to what happened and why, and support your own anger with the documented facts of the situation.

Once you get your anger out, you can forgive, forget, and get on with the business of living. Remember that anger doesn't have to be just or unjust—it's an emotion. Emotions are not always logical, so don't waste time wondering whether your anger was justified or brooding about what else you might have said or done.

On the other hand, there are going to be many times in your life when you're on the *receiving* instead of the giving end of anger, and obviously it's just as important to keep the proper perspective when you're dealing with someone else's emotions. Many women freeze in the face of another's rage because anger is equated with parental disapproval and the feeling of having done something wrong. Remember that as an adult you are the judge of your own behavior; the other person's rage is not your responsibility. However, you *do* want to understand exactly what the problem is all about. Questions requiring objective answers can trigger the other person's thinking process and get the conversation away from the emotional level and back to the intellectual level.

It also helps to remember that an angry voice cannot hurt you. Some women are able to simply listen, without feeling that they must retaliate or soothe. If you find that you're falling apart, simply excuse yourself. Let the person know that you want to work the problem out, but you are unable to reason with him when he is out of control. When you're both calm, you'll have a much better chance of getting to the root of the difficulty.

Dealing directly with your own anger and with that of another person is the prerequisite for all emotionally honest relationships. And they're the only ones that count. Once you've learned how to recognize your anger, and how to express it at both a primitive and a social level, your health *and* your performance at work will show the difference. Anger *is* good for you.

CHAPTER *8*

Personal Power

———————

Your personal power is the most important part of your overall identity. It gives you a sense of well-being that allows you to act effectively, to exert authority and dominance, and to control and influence others. Personal power closes the gap between the effect you want to give in a specific situation and the effect you actually give.

Feeling your personal power can make you come alive—yet many women refuse to accept the fact that having a sense of power can be a positive experience. They fear power because they believe it will make them unfeminine; they see powerful people as people who are inconsiderate of others. So they give their power away. The helplessness that results was summed up by one woman in therapy, "I feel as if I'm standing on the edge of the ocean of life with the waves of other people's opinions and demands rolling over me and knocking me down." She has given her power away.

You probably started giving your power away when you were a child. You did something you knew was wrong and then ran to your mother, crying, "My brother made me do it." Back then it may have been spilling the milk, kicking the baby, or letting the dog out of the backyard, but by adult life you had moved on to saying, "You made me feel angry"—or sick, or depressed, or upset, or miserable. You're making another person responsible for your feelings.

Some women give away their personal power by saying "If it hadn't been for you, I would have been rich," or famous, or married. That's simply not true. Nobody can control your life unless *you* allow it. If you *do* allow it, you're setting yourself up for powerlessness and helplessness. Powerful people don't blame others. They know what's their responsibility and what's the other person's responsibility.

Whenever you say "You made me" you're giving your power away in exchange for trying to make the other person feel guilty. That kind of an exchange is not fair to him or good for you because you're saying that he, not you, has the power to make you experience an emotional feeling. Other people can only *contribute* to your feelings; they can't *control* them.

Think of another person as an environment, just like a place. You may choose to avoid the seashore if you sunburn easily, and in the same way you may choose to avoid a particular person if you have bad feelings when you're with him. Use the reference point of how you feel when you're with the people in your life; you may find that you need to reevaluate some of your relationships.

Peggy met her older sister for lunch every week, and dutifully listened as her sister told her all the things she was handling improperly. By the time lunch was over Peggy felt totally inadequate, yet she always returned for more negative feedback the next week. At Florence's workshop, Peggy realized that she needed to change her relationship with her sister either by confronting her or by seeing her less often.

In Celia's case, the solution was more drastic. She and a friend had started a small consignment business distributing hand-made skirts to local specialty shops. After the novelty of the business wore off, Celia discovered that she was doing all the work—and listening to her friend make excuses. Celia felt abused until she ended the association and found a new partner who was willing to do her share.

In many instances, women allow the way they feel to be dictated by their relationship with a particular man. They give their power away to the man who makes them feel happy, forgetting that he can also make them feel miserable. At times, an insecure man will feel threatened by the thought that you might surpass him, and he'll try to keep you in a helpless position. Jackie remembers all the attention her male friend paid her while she was desperately trying to cram for her bar exams. He insisted that she rest from her studying with dinners at fancy French restaurants and walks in the park—until Jackie woke up to the fact that he was unconsciously trying to keep her from studying.

It's a good idea to question a person who *always* seems to want to help you. It may be that the person he really wants to help is himself. Jane, a commercial artist, was flattered by the amount of time a particular art director spent on her projects. She thought that he believed in her creative ability and would advance her cause at his ad agency. In fact, he was simply enjoying the admiration of a woman fifteen years his junior. He didn't plan to help her professionally, nor did he believe that she was any more talented than the other artists with whom he worked.

Of course, it isn't realistic to think that you'll be able to rid yourself of *all* the negative relationships in your life—there will always be *somebody* who's rotten, mean, or nasty. But you *will* need to deal with your feelings about people like this. For example, if you work for a boss who practices management by exception, mentioning only errors and never praising you, try to get him to clarify the jobs that you *are* performing well. If his lack of praise for a job well done has made you feel inadequate, begin your new personal power approach to your life by processing those emotional feelings intellectually. You can be the judge of your own performance. You don't need somebody else's praise to do a good job because you can compliment yourself.

———————

If you've been giving away your personal power, you must begin to reclaim it by assuming responsibility for yourself. Start with the most basic expressions of your feelings by saying, for instance, "I feel sick when you yell at me," instead of "You *make* me feel sick."

Marjorie, a workshop participant, always blamed her feelings on others. She told the group that her friends made her feel depressed about her low-paying job. At the end of the workshop, she participated in a role play with another member, who said sweetly, "I'm sorry I've made you depressed again." Marjorie, who had appeared timid and shy—and powerless—startled the group by banging her fist on the desk and responding, "I own my depression. It's *mine*, not yours. I'm choosing to be depressed today, and I may choose something else tomorrow." Marjorie had made a start in reclaiming her personal power. Soon it would carry beyond the supportive atmosphere of the workshop and into her relationships.

Each time you hear yourself make a strong positive statement about yourself you increase your power quotient and your personal potency. A powerful person knows that only *she* knows how she feels. She doesn't let somebody else tell her. If a person tries to tell you how you feel, stop him, challenge him, and ask him to explain exactly why he's come to those conclusions.

Of course, there are certain times in everybody's life when they must temporarily relinquish control to another person. The accountant who prepares your income tax and the lawyer who negotiates your divorce settlement are controlling your life, but if they function poorly you can always choose to fire them. You retain your personal power because you control their impact on your life. Remember that nobody can stay in your life if it's your choice to get rid of them. The only person who stays with you is *you*.

Everybody has personal power. Some people also have *formal* power, the kind of power that goes with a job. Formal power should simply allow you to get the people who work for you to do their jobs effectively. Unfortunately, many people overextend their formal power and use it inappropriately. For example, you don't need to throw your weight around or exert power over someone who's clearly your subordinate or someone who isn't responsible for a certain problem.

Secretaries often come up against the inappropriate use of formal power. "What good does it do," asks one secretary, "for someone to scold *me* when they're calling my boss about a problem? There are times when I can do something to help, but not when I'm approached like that."

You may not have a job that includes formal power, but you always have the personal power that comes from being in charge of yourself. Maintaining that power is a daily job, particularly if you've fallen into the habit of blaming others for whatever goes wrong in your life. Personal power is *yours* as soon as you take the responsibility for your feelings and choices and accept the consequences.

The lines between formal power and personal power may often blur. Your formal power comes from the fact that someone works for you, but it won't help your working relationship to say, "I'm the boss, so you'd better have that order filled by five o'clock." Instead, your personal power, used to acknowledge an employee's value and worth, helps to establish the kind of working relationship in which a job is done properly and on time.

Back in 1927, in one of the earliest studies in motivational research, Western Electric discovered that praise and appreciation are often the best ways to get a job done. Researchers chose a group of employees and studied their output under a variety of circumstances. They changed the lighting and the temperature, repainted the factory walls, and added a coffee machine. After each change, production increased. Finally the researchers determined that it was the *attention*, not the extras, that made the difference.

Sometimes personal power involves knowing when to say, "I'm one of you" instead of "I'm different from you." You'll have better luck getting a policy passed by a board if you create the feeling that you care about the same issues they do, instead of presenting yourself as an expert who's telling them what to do.

The key is in the effect you want to give, and powerful people are very aware of the impression they're conveying. You must know your audience before you can approach it in a powerful fashion—accountants will check your figures, management people will check your efficiency, and psychologists will judge you by the way you come across. An authority position will be the most effective approach when you're chairing a meeting, but you'll get a lot farther in sales if you're open and friendly.

A professional fund raiser recalls an experience many years ago when he had to call on the female vice president of a telephone company. He was new to this kind of work and unused to dealing with liberated women; he had no idea whether to call the woman Miss, Mrs., or Ms. (and he wasn't even sure how to pronounce the latter). His uncertainty and apprehension vanished when she walked out of her office, smiled, and said, "I'm

Ann, you must be Dave." He remembers that her greeting immediately put him at ease. "Women have a lot of quiet power going for them," he says. "As soon as they realize it, they'll be running the country."

———————•—•—•———————

Personal power on the job also comes from having the basic skills required for your work. Obviously, you'll feel more powerful if you know you don't have to cover up for yourself. If your job requires typing and you're a poor typist, take a typing class at a local night school. If you must write business reports, sign up for a course in business writing. If you keep getting off on the wrong foot with coworkers, enroll in a communications workshop. Personal power is always enhanced by recognizing a weakness and then taking the necessary steps to improve it. If you don't have all the skills you think you need, start making plans to acquire them.

You won't be running behind trying to catch up if you've learned the cultural, sexual, and regional variations involved in a particular job. If certain people prefer to do business in a certain way—bargaining over prices, say—then you should know how to do it their way; if you're dealing with a female manager, then you might reasonably expect her to have a slightly different perspective in some areas than a man would; if you're working in the South or the Midwest, you can expect the pace and style to differ from that in New York or California.

A market researcher from the East who spent some time working in Texas had this reaction to the change in locale: "When a New York boss tells you that he wants a report he means that he wants it yesterday, but in Texas the same report is expected in three weeks. There it's a mistake to do things too quickly because you aren't meeting the norm. Your coworkers will feel threatened."

Of course, differences in pace and style may occur even in a small area. A teacher recalls that the three different schools in her town, separated by five miles, seemed light years away from each other. The children in the school that bordered a steel mill were from blue-collar families. Their principal ran his school in a rigid, old-fashioned style. Just two miles away, where the student body consisted of the children of professional people, the school had open classrooms. The third school, right outside the city limit, had an entirely different atmosphere. The children came from the old, established families, and the style was more like that of a prep school.

————— •◦• —————

Your personal power also requires knowing which hat to wear in each situation you'll encounter in a business day. You may need to be an executive, a salesperson, and a counselor within the space of a few hours! Each role requires a different presentation because their effects are all different. A middle manager in a corporation explains it this way: "This morning I reviewed a performance appraisal with one of my employees. I functioned as his boss when I told him which skills he needed to improve, but as a salesman for my company when I urged him to stay instead of taking a job on the West Coast. I wound up the conference as a counselor, listening to him talk about his divorce settlement. Then I had a meeting with my own boss to push for the allocation of an extra $100,000 for a project. After that, my management trainee, a seventeen-year-old high school student, asked to see me. His father had just abandoned the family, and he was afraid of shouldering the new responsibility. As you can see, I'm continually shifting gears."

————— •◦• —————

Personal power may be divided into *internal* and *external* power. If you haven't considered yourself a powerful person in

A Comparison of Powerful and Powerless Looks

	Powerful	**Powerless**
Clothes	Tailored suit with blazer jacket	Dress with frills
Overcoat	Wrap-around camel coat	Flaired coat
Raincoat	Trench coat, umbrella	Poncho, plastic rain hat, shawl
Purse	Attache case or small clutch bag	Large, floppy bag
Jewelry	Round gold hoop necklace; large watch & ring; simple post or ball earrings	Anything dangling
Hair	Slightly short to medium length	Very long or very short
Make-up	Moderately dark lashes; precisely & moderately shaped eyebrows; slight cheek color; moderate color lipstick	Large false eyelashes; very thin eyebrows; heavy, red rouge; no lipstick

the past, you may need to start building your powerful image from the outside by using dress, body language, and communication techniques that will reinforce the new attitudes you're trying to build on the inside.

Powerful people know that first impressions always count. Many business situations involve strangers, who have no idea how effective you're going to be. That first impression will make the difference in whether they get an opportunity to find out. *You are what you pretend to be.* When you come across in a businesslike fashion, you're treated that way. And the more you're treated like a businesswoman, the more secure you'll become in that role—until one day you won't be pretending any more.

You can project an image of personal power by the way you dress. John T. Molloy's *The Woman's Dress For Success Book* reinforces many of Florence's observations about the importance of clothing, particularly the idea that dressing to succeed in business and dressing to be sexually attractive are mutually exclusive. It's taken you a long time to travel from the little woman in the kitchen to the power-monger in the office, and if you turn up in a sexy outfit you'll destroy an image you've worked hard to create.

All of your clothing should be well cut because a clean visual line gives an impression of organization, while the frilly feminine look suggests clutter and disorganization. Remember that the clean, straight lines of a businessman's suit inspire confidence and make him appear businesslike before he even opens his mouth.

If you'll be outside a lot, adopt a hair style that won't suffer. Ruth, a million-dollar real estate saleswoman, got a wash-and-wear haircut that didn't mind the rain because she shows property in all kinds of weather. "If you want to be successful in real estate you need to cultivate a personal appearance that doesn't take a lot of fuss. I can't run for cover if I want to make a sale."

She tries to adapt her clothing to the kind of property she's selling—tweeds for the country and suits for town.

While you're concentrating on appearances, don't forget how your *office* looks. You can make your office look as powerful as you do. Include a large but not overwhelming chair and pictures of your children, but not your husband.

If you don't have an office, you can still make a less-defined space look like it's yours by marking your territory with a poster or positioning your desk in a slightly different way. Keeping your desk clean and well organized will also help create a powerful first impression.

Along with your choice of clothing and office decor, your body language will create an image of quiet personal power. In fact, your body language may tell your coworkers a lot more about you than you think—and maybe more than you'd like them to know. Body language, or nonverbal communication, is a new science, and many experts disagree on the findings. No one sign has only one interpretation. For example, scratching your nose may mean that you're disapproving, but it may also just mean that you have an itch or want to sneeze. However, even though you realize that there aren't any absolutes of meaning in body language it can still become an effective tool.

There's nothing new about nonverbal communication. Your body has been relaying messages ever since you were little. Just think back a minute. Couldn't your mother tell that something was wrong by the way you stood or squirmed? Perhaps you blinked, covered your mouth with your hand, or stared at your feet. She may not have known what you'd done, but she *did* know that it wasn't good.

Now that you're an adult, you can communicate personal power by your body language. The powerful person walks into a room standing straight with her head up. She seeks eye con-

A Comparison of Powerful and Powerless Body Language

	Powerful	**Powerless**
Posture	Stand straight, erect, with shoulders back	Slouch, hold head down, with back hunched
Eye contact	Look the other person in the eye, but don't stare or look too long	Quick eye contact, then look away or down
Hands	When standing, held loosely at your sides; when sitting, hands in front of you, with elbows resting on your desk, arms up, fingers interwoven slightly	Fidget and move excessively
Feet	When standing, balance on both feet; when sitting, cross the legs at the knee	When standing, shift weight from one foot to other; when sitting, cross legs at ankles, spread legs, rock and swing feet, and tap feet

tact, chooses a chair close to the speaker, and introduces herself immediately. She sits relaxed, with her hands in her lap. She is free of nervous, fidgety gestures. The powerless person knocks timidly at the door, and waits hesitantly until she's invited in. A powerless person always needs instructions. She walks slowly and chooses a chair that's removed from the group and looks to the others to speak and to invite her to introduce herself. She looks down and avoids eye contact. Her nervous gestures include fidgeting and clutching her arms across her chest. While the powerful person brings life and energy into a meeting simply by her presence, the powerless person will drain a conversation. In fact, one wants to get rid of her quickly.

Let's take a look at the nonverbal communication that may go on at a routine sales meeting. The district manager may stand, since standing is a power position. He strides back and forth beside a blackboard. His walk communicates his state of mind—powerless people walk with their heads down and their hands in their pockets, while powerful people stride energetically along with their hands on their hips. According to Calero and Nierenberg's *How To Read a Person Like a Book*, people who are preoccupied with a problem tend to keep their heads down and their hands locked behind their backs. They look up when the problem is solved.

The district manager might have adopted the seated position of equality if he didn't plan to chew out his staff. A look at the position of the feet under the conference table will tell him how his staff is reacting to his lecture. If the feet are together and turned slightly, it may mean that the person is paying attention but isn't willing to commit himself to a new policy. If the knees are parallel but to one side, he's listening but may not be ready to make a decision. Knees held tightly together are apt to mean that he's opposed. Get the idea?

Before leaving the subject of body language, stop to consider the one gesture that does more than almost any other to communicate your personal power—the handshake. Handshaking is a major hurdle for women starting out in business. Little boys are brought up shaking hands, but little girls spend their formative years smiling, kissing cheeks, and giving an occasional curtsy, none of which are terribly appropriate for the business world. A personnel director has noticed that women in their thirties and forties tend to bring their social manners to a business interview, and avoid shaking hands. "Women feel awkward about shaking hands, but they feel worse if I put my hand out and they don't. Making a mistake like that at the beginning of an interview really gets them off on the wrong foot." She suggests that women who plan to enter the job market practice shaking hands by approaching all contacts, both social and professional, with a handshake—until sticking out their hand has become automatic.

———————

Personal power comes from knowing what's expected of you in a certain situation and being comfortable doing it. And there are certain communication techniques that you can use to help yourself along.

You may need to assert your dominance to get an idea accepted. In this case, you might try using the "mirror" technique. Psychologists have found that we unconsciously identify with people who seem to have the same qualities we have, and mirroring is a good way to establish that common bond without having to say a word.

Grace worked for a social service agency. Her boss was preparing the new budget and had gotten the staff members together to go over the expenditures for the past year. Fundraising for the programs had not been completely successful, and she was upset that she would have to present a deficit to her board. Grace immediately picked up her boss's fear and vulnerability and mirrored her concern at the meeting, leaning forward slightly whenever her boss did, gently drumming her fingers on the table when her boss did, and nodding her head. Throughout the meeting her boss continually turned to her for agreement. During that meeting, Grace successfully forged a common bond with her boss.

Another way to take a dominant position is to stand over another person. Elevation has always signified superiority. God is usually depicted as living "on high"; judges sit in elevated places and "hand down" their decision. Such phrases as "put her on a pedestal" or "look up to him" infer the belief that height and dominance go together.

As we mentioned before, we all are sensitive to intrusions on our personal space. The term "territoriality" indicates your ownership and thus dominance over a certain space. Social scientist Robert Ardrey claims that territoriality is genetic and that each of us is born with a need to own our space. When you move into another person's personal space he may fight to defend it. A businessman who maintains an office in his home admits that he feels almost violent when he sees somebody sitting at his desk. "I can feel discomfort welling up inside of me, and I start yelling the second I walk into the room."

Personal space—the area around you that you see as yours—can be different for different people. For example, Florence has found that violent people need more space around them than nonviolent people. Whatever a person's orientation, dominance can occur when someone intrudes on an individual's personal space. Imagine that you're sitting at your desk when suddenly your boss comes into the office and stands over your desk, waving a report and saying that you've done it all wrong. You feel anxious and upset, and you believe that those feelings are generated by the fact that you *did* do a poor job. Naturally, some of your anxiety is related to the rebuke, but another part comes from the fact that the boss is violating your personal space.

Personal Power

Your office and your desk are *your* territory, and you can *extend* your territory by placing objects on additional space. For example, a student who doesn't want to be disturbed while studying in the library may spread his books out around him on the table. A theatergoer may throw his coat over the chair beside him if he doesn't want somebody to sit there. In the same way, putting your feet on your desk or leaning against your car indicate dominance and ownership. In social situations, a husband may put his arm around his wife's shoulders or hold her hand to indicate that she "belongs" to him.

———•·——

Personal power and communication go hand in hand because in order to feel powerful you must have developed not only the ability to *receive* accurate information, but also the ability to *express yourself* in return. Obviously, communication takes place on *many* levels. If you're unsure of your verbal skills, it often helps to plot out your message beforehand, without the use of opinions or judgements. Use a simple diagram for communicating facts:

Subject	Verb	Description	Reason
The report	is due	Thursday	to meet the funding deadline.

When you want to communicate the way you feel, state the feeling, followed by why—if you choose to. You might say "I feel happy because I was promoted." But remember that nobody can *tell* you how you feel.

Powerful people are comfortable giving orders. They tell clearly what needs to be done, when, and how. They may give their reasons, depending on the relationship and the situation. They always acknowledge and consider the other person, but they maintain their own responsibility for giving orders.

If you have difficulty giving orders, try using the following formula:

Tell what needs to be done	*When*	*How*	*Why*	*Acknowledge other person.*
I want this report typed.	By 5 PM Friday.	Double spaced, in triplicate.	A client needs to take it to a conference.	Thank you.

Your personal power is going to come from generating power *attitudes* to go along with your new wardrobe, body language, and communication skills. Powerful people don't assume that other people will guess what they want them to do. They tell them whatever they need to know. Powerful people don't repeat things unless they're asked, and they don't list a lot of reasons why they can't do something. Usually they just figure out a way to do it. If they've exhausted all other possibilities, they'll simply admit what they can't do and why, and go on to the next challenge.

There is power in what you say, and there's also power in *how* you say it. You have power in your voice when you state facts clearly and concisely in a moderate but firm tone. Emphasize appropriate words, concentrate on a smooth delivery, and pause for attention. Avoid a whiney, high-pitched sound; a harsh, hard, tight voice; a monotone; or those gosh, gee, uhs that go with many hesitations. Use a tape recorder to listen to your voice.

And listen to *other* people too. Effective listening projects as much personal power as speaking. Make sure that you have the time to listen, then pay attention to the person, look at him, listen to the content of what he's saying, and watch his body signals. Do they match or contradict his words?

If you don't have time to listen when first approached, be sure to arrange *another* time. Don't interrupt someone who's talking to you. Don't finish his sentences for him or interject your own thoughts before he finishes. Remember that his feelings cannot be legislated, so don't tell him that he shouldn't feel a particular way. Instead ask him *why* he feels the way he does.

Powerful people develop the powerful attitude of thinking that they're two steps farther up the business ladder than they actually are. You're a secretary who's going to *stay* a secretary if you're preoccupied with typing and filing, answering the telephone and making appointments. But if you're a secretary who thinks about herself as a potential boss, you'll begin to study the way your boss does things, and learn the way your boss addresses a problem.

Remember that your job is what you're investing your time in, so do your best to make it a positive and creative experience. You may not like being a receptionist, but it's one rung on that corporate ladder and, like all the others, it can lead to the top. You're the first person the public meets, so you're a saleswoman and an ambassador. Dress for the job, greet the public, and notice how your company works, what their visitors are like, and who is considered important. You'll soon be recognized as a valuable—and promotable—employee.

———•—•———

Personal power brings freedom. Nobody has undue influence over the powerful person. When you begin to feel your own power you'll discard those dependent needs that get you into trouble and turn you into a victim. You won't need to be flattered, smiled at, or have yes-men all around you. Those needs make you susceptible to manipulation by people who tell you what you want to hear—for their gain, not yours.

Your personal power gives you the freedom to realize that you don't need one specific person, job, or thing in your life. There are many jobs and many people to choose from, and the powerful person doesn't get hung up on the idea that there's just *one* choice.

A powerful person doesn't need to be constantly appreciated or rewarded, and doesn't need to bluff. A powerful person also knows that she cannot be threatened. If somebody tells you that he'll quit, fire you, cost you money, or sue you, you should be able to rationally consider the consequences. Your ability to do this immediately destroys your opponent's leverage.

Powerful people create an atmosphere that reflects their personality; they feel good about themselves, are flexible, and say what they mean. They are able to evaluate an act, and can distinguish between a person and his actions. Anyone who *has* personal power knows that it's the passport to successful living both at home and at work.

CHAPTER 9

Who's Boss in the Office Family?

There's nothing really new about your office family. It's filled with the same varied personalities, resentments, and jealousies as your biological one. And, just like life with your family, the office experience isn't always going to be a positive one. You'll find that you'll meet up with warm, caring people as well as cold, critical ones. Remember that your growth as a person who is able to take care of herself emotionally comes from both positive *and* negative experiences. They're the yardstick by which you can measure your own development. Naturally, you're not going to seek out the negative influences at the office any more than you might choose to live next door to a relative you dislike, but you're not going to run away from them either.

Laurie is her company's first female manager, and she's met with resistance from both the men and the women working for her. "In the beginning, the women resented me because they were used to having a man as their leader. His authority was acceptable, but mine wasn't. The men didn't like working for a woman. They felt that it demeaned their status to have a female boss—almost as if they were back with their mother again. I decided to prove myself to both my employees and my superiors, who were watching me closely, by emphasizing my competence instead of my sex. I reorganized the department and added job incentives and training programs. Before too long, people were asking to be transferred *into* my department. It had become known as the training ground for young executives."

Laurie has succeeded in coping with a number of obstacles in her office family. In doing so, she's developed her own style of leadership—a major feat for many women, who've spent their lives as followers. Instead of waiting to be told how to solve her department's morale problem, Laurie took action herself and initiated a new method of working, which her employees respected.

Like Laurie, you'll be able to work with anybody as long as you're comfortable with yourself and your feelings. There will be many times at work when you'll be better off in a negative situation because it's still the best learning situation. And if you're the boss, you may have to discover ways to convince some of your employees that what *they* think is a bad situation is actually a good one. Whatever side of the fence you're on, you'll be better able to cope if you understand the differences between the ways men and women behave with members of their *own* sex and the *opposite* sex.

———————

Occasionally women who are unfamiliar with the business scene stay in a bad job because they're afraid they can't get another one, or because they get used to their boss's peculiarities. "I didn't realize how strange my boss really was or how poorly she managed her department until she had an emergency operation and was out of the office for six weeks," says a young woman who found that her boss's replacement had a much different style. If *you're* stuck with a bad boss, you'll need to assess what you're getting out of the relationship other than punishment. If you're learning something you might decide to stay—but only until you have what you need.

Who's Boss in the Office Family?

The real issue with any boss is not his or her sex, but his or her competence. A good boss is secure in his or her job and able to give you the direction you need by establishing guidelines and setting standard procedures. A good boss will stick up for you and push you ahead in the company. A good boss uses the group in the office, delegates responsibility to others, is consistent, and allows people the time to do their job without looking over their shoulders. "My first boss was so afraid that I wouldn't meet my deadlines that she stood over me, nagged, and took up so much of my time that I almost didn't," says a copywriter. "The best boss I ever had established deadlines and then left us alone to meet them, but checked regularly to see if we needed any help. He was always there if needed, but he didn't look over your shoulder or criticize until the end." He understood the business process.

One of the most common male-female relationships at the office is the paternalistic boss who sees his female employees as daughter figures. His socialization has led him to take a protective attitude towards women. Consciously or unconsciously, they often respond in kind.

"I know that my women prefer having a male boss so that they can get the paternalistic thing going," says an assembly line supervisor. "Remember that women were once daughters, they often had special feelings for their father—he was the final authority." This man feels that he gets on better with his female employees than with the males, who are more apt to challenge his authority.

Although he often gives his employees a lot of encouragement, a paternalistic boss may not be a lot of help if you want to get ahead. George saw the younger women in his department very much the way he saw his own daughters. One young woman spent several years as his assistant, and he urged that she be promoted. But he made sure that the promotion kept her in his orbit, and even though she had some responsibility he protected her from any real risks in the company, which in turn kept her from having any *real* learning experiences. Everyone else in the department knows that George's protegé is incapable of making any important decision without consulting him, and none of her colleagues take her seriously.

It's also a good idea not to become too indispensable to your boss. He can become just as dependent on you as you are on him. "One day I realized that losing me would be a serious blow for my boss. We worked well together and I was valuable to him because I often knew what was happening in the company before he did. I was afraid that he might not want to promote me, so I took the problem to him directly and told him that in order to maintain my independence I ought to work in another department. I asked him to help me find another job. At first he was surprised and disappointed that I wanted to leave, but since he had always been paternalistic, he went to bat for me and found me a better job in the personnel department."

Remember that a paternalistic boss *does* want to help you. If you get angry, he's likely to be confused and hurt. On the other hand, if you plot your career path in advance and take the time to assess your situation at regular intervals, you won't allow yourself to settle into a comfortable, cozy relationship in which further growth may be impossible. Beware of what one employment counselor calls a woman's "nesting instinct."

On the other hand, some women take advantage of a paternalistic boss. Ben liked the casual, family atmosphere in his business, until he realized that his female employees were bringing all of their personal problems to his desk. "I woke up to the fact that I was neither their shrink nor their big brother. I was running a business. My employees would just have to get their emotional relief elsewhere." Having made this decision he was able to clarify his relationship with his employees. Ben had discovered a primary rule in all office relationships—know yourself *first*, know what you will and will not accept, because other people are going to take *their* direction from you.

Monitor your own behavior to see whether or not you fall back on the traditional female stereotypes. This kind of behavior can be a real problem for any boss. One executive says that he dreads having a conference with one of his female employees and must steel himself for the confrontation, which is usually more emotional than rational.

Mary, a personnel director, explains just how frustrating this kind of behavior can be. "Our procedure for hourly employees starts with a verbal warning, followed by a written warning, after which I sit down with the supervisor and the employee. If she doesn't improve, she's given a one-week suspension without pay. If she *still* doesn't shape up, I have to fire her. There are times when I feel like shaking an employee who bursts into tears and tries to use emotion on me after three opportunities to do better."

You can also gain insight into your relationship with your boss by comparing it with the one you had with your parents. The odds are that there are a lot of similarities. If you got along well with your parents and had little difficulty accepting their authority, you'll probably have that same easy working relationship with your boss, but if you resented authority as a child you may discover that you're setting up power plays with your boss. If you were a good little girl who was afraid of making a mistake and displeasing your parents, you may be the kind of employee who drives the boss crazy because you're afraid to think or act independently. Your working relationship will improve as soon as you recognize that outdated emotional baggage and leave it at home where it belongs.

————————

Although many studies have reported that women dislike having a female boss, it's recently come to light that the majority of those studies were performed on women who had never actually *worked* for a female boss. They were simply imagining.

Many women who *have* female bosses are discovering that they can add a new dimension of understanding and compassion to a job. The recognition of women's issues that began in consciousness-raising groups in the early '70s has strengthened over the years and brought women closer together. On the job and at home they've worked together to get a fair deal from men. They're trusting each other on new turf instead of competing with each other on the old.

In many cases, a solidarity exists between the women in an office. A publishing executive says the young women in her company stuck together when they realized that young men joined the firm at higher job levels, were paid more, and were given promotions more quickly. When a new job opened up, the women tended to lobby *first* for the management's acknowledgement that a woman should get the position—only then would they consider each other as competitors for the new spot.

A woman's nurturing qualities and her preference for close one-to-one relationships may help her subordinates. Corporate middle managers often work so closely and effectively with their secretaries that the secretaries usually advance quickly to better positions. "My boss was interested in me as a person as well as in the way I performed my job," said one secretary. "She taught me about the company and inspired me to perform at my peak efficiency. After I was promoted, I realized that I had been too dependent on her and had worked for *her* rather than for my career. My new job requires that I make many independent decisions, but I'm discovering just how well my first boss prepared me for the new responsibility." Her boss explains their relationship by remarking that she sees her employees as people with whom she shares a common female psychology.

According to social scientist Dr. Ann Beuf, women actually work the most effectively and produce the best results when they're in a *totally* female group. This is largely due to the fact that their productivity is not influenced by competition for the attention of a man, or seeing themselves as the followers of a man. In a mixed group, women may not fulfill their work potential because they become listeners—the men do the talking.

Of course, not every woman-to-woman relationship works. The female boss may be a "Queen Bee" who's excessively picky and wants to have everything under her control. She *says* she's open to suggestions, but she rarely takes them because she likes to be in the limelight all by herself. You may feel more like her slave than her employee. A newspaper woman who is now an editor describes her "Queen Bee" this way: "My first boss was a tyrant who even expected me to run her personal errands. She tried to regulate both my clothing and my choice of friends. Most of the time I couldn't stand her, and I'd never put up with that kind of relationship again—but she was teaching me a lot about the newspaper business that I didn't think I could learn any other way. I stuck it out until I had learned all I could and had enough clippings to move on to a better job. I might have done that much sooner if I hadn't been young, dependent, and unsure."

The boss who elects to be your office mother may succeed in sapping your own initiative. Don't let it happen. "My boss checked up on everything we did and hung over our shoulders so that we wouldn't make a mistake," says a graphics designer. "We began to rely more and more on her. Why should we work so hard if she was going to redo everything anyway? The only opinion in the office that counted was hers." The boss probably was no happier with this situation than the mother who finds that her children are leaving more and more of the chores for her to do, simply because she continues to do them. The new female boss needs to learn to delegate authority and treat her employees as individuals, not as children reflecting on a parent.

Some of the new woman manager's problems come from her own insecurity on the job. In many cases, her promotion occurs before she's ready and before she's spent enough time in lower-level positions to learn the ins and outs of the way her company works. In *The Managerial Woman,* Hennig and Jardim draw attention to the differences between new male and female managers. A man wonders how he can put together an effective department, while a woman worries about herself. Can she do the job that she's been promoted to do? Her inward preoccupation dulls her outward objectivity, and she sees her team simply in terms of its impact on her ability to do *her* job. She feels that she must prove herself to justify her promotion.

Too often these days a woman reaches a managing position and discovers she has nobody to turn to for advice. She doesn't ask questions because she's afraid of showing her ignorance, and this blocks her ability to learn. "A man expects to learn on the job, but a woman thinks she's just supposed to *know,*" says one executive. He's noticed that women department heads often try to learn everything about the company themselves, while the men only learn who to ask. A woman complicates her job unnecessarily because she's insecure.

Sometimes a woman doesn't delegate authority because she's afraid she'll lose control of her department; she's afraid that if one of her people makes a mistake it will reflect on her ability as a manager. In many cases, her insecurity keeps her from hiring the very people who'll help her department run more smoothly. She may avoid highly competent females for fear they'll take *her* job.

"Learning to be a boss can be a full-time job in itself," says an editor who remembers that her own transition from secretary

150

to editor was a difficult one. She shared a secretary with two other junior editors, and at first she was embarrassed to ask her to do "boring" chores because she somehow felt that she had to give her "interesting" work. She wasn't able to separate her former interests as a secretary from her new ones as a boss.

A college professor sums up her difficulty dealing with secretaries this way: "Women haven't been trained to exploit people the way men have, and they haven't watched too many other women handle a secretary. Older secretaries can be a particular problem for women because they tend to treat them like mothers." Like the editor, she vascillated between giving her secretary too much work and too little until she finally became comfortable in her new job and developed her own style.

Lack of information networks with their peers may also leave working women vulnerable. "Even when women *do* get together they're not as apt to talk shop as men are," says an employment counselor. "They have fewer reference points." They wouldn't be so hurt by changes in office relationships if they had more feedback. This a particularly true in the shift from employee to supervisor.

As a legal secretary in a large law firm, Fay enjoyed regular lunches with several other secretaries. Then she was tapped as an employee with higher-level potential and given a new job as an administrative assistant. She expected to have her new office, new salary, and expanded responsibility—and lunch with her friends. Instead she ate alone. "I still remember the first day. I sat in my fancy office and waited for the girls to tell me they were leaving for lunch. Finally I came out and realized that they'd gone without me. I was no longer one of the group." Women band together and enjoy the company of their equals at work. In the beginning, Fay ate lunch alone in her office because the men didn't include her either. But Fay was patient and eventually began lunching with the men. She had discovered that every office has its hierarchy.

Ellen had a more difficult time when she became a supervisor. She had worked for a year in the central supply department of a hospital. At fifty-three she was the unofficial mother of the six other women in the department, who were all in their twenties and thirties. When the hospital expanded, she was the obvious choice for supervisor. She was happy about her promotion not only because she needed the extra money, but also because she thought she'd get still closer to her young friends in the department. How wrong she was. "I went through hell. The girls didn't want to work under supervision. In the past, I'd only been responsible for *my* work, but now I had to keep tabs on theirs. They took lengthy coffee breaks and lunch hours, and often mixed up the equipment and sent it to different floors just to get me in trouble. I took everything they did personally and became hurt and angry. Then my boss helped me to see that it wasn't *me* but my new authority that they resented." Even though the department is running smoothly now, Ellen is looking for a new job. She wants whatever she does to have a close one-to-one quality, the kind of relationship she had in her department before she became supervisor.

Ellen's experience is a reminder of a fact many working women find hard to accept: there should be different levels of friendship at home and in the office. You'll need a few close friends with whom you can share your personal life, but these friends don't always belong at the office. In the same way, leisure-time friends with whom you engage in hobbies and sports can be on a different level from your intimate friends or your business associates.

Above all, a boss is not a buddy or a best friend. A boss can counsel and advise a subordinate on how to advance in a corporation and can serve as a mentor by opening the right doors, but a boss will lose her control if she becomes too much of a pal. The proper relationship between a boss and a subordinate is cemented by mutual respect for each other's abilities—for their professionalism.

It's likely that a man in management will have had this sort of mentor-pupil relationship. An older man in the company will teach him the ropes, push him ahead, and look out for him. Many women don't have mentors. They're only just beginning to reach the levels at which they can be supportive and helpful to *other* women in their company. In many cases, they haven't been aware of the informal network of knowledge and contacts that men have used for years. With the growth of the women's movement, women have become more conscious of their responsibility to each other. The strong corporate woman can be the catalyst for other women in her company.

Doris is a well-paid executive in the human resources department of her corporation. She pushes women into the limelight whenever possible. "I insist that all departments select women for executive training sessions and I work individually with the women in the corporation, outlining their career options. I make a point of only hiring women for my department who are as capable as I am and who can do my job as well or better. No, I'm not scared of the competition because I'm confident in my own ability and I want to hire the kind of women who will become mentors for *other* women in the company. Women need to look at *women* in upper-level positions so that they really believe that they can do it too."

———————•—•———————

Even if she can handle the requirements of her new job, the new supervisor may find that her male employees are resentful. You'll have an easier time if you're sensitive to a man's dislike of taking orders from a woman. A bookstore manager recalls that she got on well with the women who worked for her, but the men, on the other hand, bridled when she gave them lists of chores or reminded them about a job. They accused her of acting like their mother.

One telephone company supervisor says that she remains somewhat detached from her male crew. She's always aware that her very presence may be the trigger for a man who's actually mad at his mother or his wife. "If I'm constantly caught up in negative behavior patterns with an employee I address the problem directly. I just tell him that I know he doesn't like working with a woman—and then we talk about it. Just stating your position often does a lot to clear the air."

One woman who supervised male engineers recalls that she had to prove she was able to do what she was asking them to do. "There was always the question of whether I, as a woman, had the proper technical ability."

At all levels, successful women recommend openly acknowledging the fact that certain male coworkers have difficulty dealing with women. "Being a woman is always an *issue,* but it isn't always a *problem,*" explains a bank executive.

Even though you're feeling comfortable at work, you'll still have to crack the male peer groups *outside* the office. The office may be the place for holding meetings and writing reports, but a lot of the *real* business goes on elsewhere. A college professor notes that the only way she could find out what was happening in her department was to join the evening poker games in the faculty lounge. "The men resented me at first because they had to clean up their language, but eventually they got used to me. You have to go to where the men go because they have a tendency to band together in groups to discuss business. If you stay in the office, you'll miss a lot of what's really going on." These kinds of informal information networks pass on such tidbits as whose project is about to be approved, who's in with the chief executive, or what policy is changing.

Many women still feel guilty about working; at five o'clock

they leave the office behind—and they're liable to miss some of the most important contacts of the day. After five, people tend to relax, and it may be easier to approach someone for advice or information. You may be invited to have a drink with some colleagues and be able to hash over the day's events or discuss an upcoming project. And by sticking around the office to finish up whatever you've been working on, you'll remind the higher-ups that you see your work the same way they do—as a career, not as a nine-to-five time-for-money exchange. One woman recalls sharing the elevator with the company president at about six one evening—and being asked to help on one of his projects the following week. He'd been curious about why she'd worked late, had asked her boss about her, and had decided to reward her efforts.

A lot of unofficial business also takes place at the bar, particularly at convention and conference time—but women are sometimes uncomfortable in a place that has traditionally been a male province. A successful realtor handles the problem this way: "I go to the bar in my most severe business outfit without any frills, since the formality has already been lessened by the fact that I'm *in* the bar. I wear my business suit and keep my business head by drinking ginger ale, and I listen to what's going on. Sometimes I rely on my sense of humor to carry me through the difficult moment of approaching a group of men who are obviously having a good time and don't particularly want to be joined. Sometimes all the talking just stops, as if I'm some sort of social curse. Then I slip into my hostess role and make them feel at home. It almost always works."

Working with men may require playing with them too at sales meetings and conventions, but there is still a different set of rules for women. Alcohol is the lubricant that keeps those business wheels turning, but a woman would be wise *never* to overindulge. A man can pass out in a stupor and come to work the next day and laugh about it, but the *woman* who gets drunk is treated in a different fashion. When your male associates get drunk, ignore it. And don't talk about it the next day either.

In the matter of office affairs, there's also a double standard for men and women. It may be okay for a man to dip his pen in the company ink, but the woman is the one who gets fired. A man who indulges in a casual affair can even be the envy of his coworkers, particularly if he snags a young girl. For a woman, the effect can be very different.

Maureen was fifteen years younger than her boss, whom she dated very discreetly. She remained strictly professional at work, and the romance might have continued for years if she and her boss had not been spotted by another employee at a local country club. The following day she lost her job. "I'm still bitter about it," she admits. "Everybody envies the guy, but they pin a scarlet letter on the girl."

Just about every woman has run across an office Romeo, the kind of man who gets his kicks from making plays for the girls at the office, who usually don't know quite how to handle his advances. It's often embarrassing to complain about something that sounds more innocent in the retelling than it was when it happened back at the coffee machine—and then there's the cloak of office cameraderie that can make a woman who complains seem prudish and standoffish.

Kristin was so repelled by her boss's advances that she complained to *his* boss. The upshot of all this was a washroom meeting in which one man slapped the other across the back and said, "Better keep your hands off Kristin, she seems to be a pretty up-tight girl—must have a problem." Her boss did keep his hands off Kristin, and he kept *Kristin* off any good public relations assignments. He told her that he didn't think she was very comfortable with men, and that she wasn't suited to public relations work. She had no choice but to quit.

Who's Boss in the Office Family?

Kristin's problem is not an uncommon one. In fact, the woman at the office often leads a double life. Her first concern is the work itself but, as Betty Harragan puts it in *Games Mother Never Taught You,* her second is a never-ending alertness to the sexual overtures of male business associates. Lin Farley, the author of *Sexual Shakedown: Sexual Harrassment of Women at Work,* testified before the New York City Commission on Human Rights that in any random group of ten working women, five to seven have had one or more experiences with unwelcome sexual advances on the job. One half to one third of all women in the work force have been affected. It's not unusual for a woman to be promised a better job in exchange for sexual favors, but recent court decisions have held that sexual harrassment is in fact a form of discrimination.

The key to dealing with this kind of behavior lies in a woman's ability to block passes while maintaining a pleasant, friendly working relationship with the men involved. Male bravado and boasting can often hide a fragile ego. The smart woman knows how to turn a man down with tact and diplomacy. She doesn't burn her bridges because yesterday's rejected lover could be tomorrow's boss.

Whether you're dealing with sexual harrassment or difficult office personalities, whether you're an employee or a boss, whether you work with many people or only a few, the bottom line of your success at work is how well you understand the people around you and why they behave the way they do. Knowing the patterns behind their relationships is an important part of this, but an equally important part is knowing *yourself.* If you're comfortable with yourself, you'll find it much easier to understand—and be comfortable with—the people you'll meet at work.

CHAPTER *10*

Competition and Teamwork

Jean attended her first competition workshop because she was disillusioned with her job at an advertising agency. She couldn't understand why the men in her department advanced and she didn't—and she blamed it on the fact that she was a woman. The truth is that Jean hasn't advanced because none of her superiors know how good she actually is. When Jean brings her ideas to a staff meeting, she finds herself deferring to others and never presents her own plans.

Dora, on the other hand, knows how to compete with men. She's a curriculum supervisor for a school board, and nobody pirates *her* plans. Even though the four male supervisors resent her presence and try to talk over her, Dora attends her meetings armed with memos, graphs, and charts. She speaks up and insists that the supervisors listen. "I don't let them shout me down, I always do my homework in advance, and I make sure that my boss gets a copy of my ideas and suggestions *before* the meeting."

Dora has been noticed as a woman with a future because she's learned how to compete with the men. Jean is treading water and getting nowhere.

Competition and Teamwork

If you want to get ahead at work you'll have to learn the habits of the working world just the way you learn the habits of any foreign country. The best European vacation is the one in which you don't feel like a tourist, and your best work performance comes when you feel like a native in the office. You may have to learn about competition and teamwork later than the men you work with, but you *can* catch up.

After all, you've been socialized since birth to avoid competition. From the time we're little girls we've been carefully taught to sit quietly in the background—not out in front. Things will be different for coming generations, but for most of today's adults the images of the ideal female and male still haven't caught up much with the changes begun by the women's movement. In fact, a study of male and female managers discovered a high correlation between their descriptions of successful middle managers and their descriptions of men in general. Only five years ago, J. H. Block's cross-cultural study of university students revealed that the men wanted to be shrewd, dominant, critical, practical, rational, and *competitive*, while the women preferred to be helpful, generous, considerate, loving, and affectionate.

Men know that competition with other people, other departments, and other companies is the bottom line of the business day, but many women are usually only familiar with one kind of competition—competing with each other for a man. Men bring a lifetime of training in competitive, aggressive behavior to the office, and women bring a lifetime of training in attending to the needs of others. It's a perfect blend for a boss-secretary relationship.

The secretary who is known as the "office wife" or "mother" is a familiar fixture at many offices. She knows her boss's moods, tells people the best way to get on his good side, and protects him from people he doesn't want to see. "We always called the boss's secretary and asked her about 'the weather'—

the boss's moods—before stopping by to see him," recalls a publishing executive. The relationship worked for years until the secretary got tired of being mother and quit.

The maternal role comes so naturally to some women that they slip into it unconsciously. "I found myself trying to make everybody comfortable at staff meetings," recalls one woman. "Then I realized that wasn't my job. If I'm going to get ahead I have to *compete* with the men not look after them." You'll have to rid yourself of this kind of behavior if *you* want to get ahead.

————————

As a little girl you were probably brought up to believe that it didn't matter whether you won or lost as long as you played a good game. Even today, it often isn't considered ladylike to *want* to win, or to come in first. The same father who commends his daughter for being a good loser may have different advice for his son—"Show me a good loser and I'll show you a loser." Boys are constantly reminded that nice guys finish last.

A little girl is encouraged to suppress the anger she feels at losing; she's told to be a good sport. Boys, on the other hand, are taught that it's okay to get angry about losing because their anger will help give them the ability to win the next time around. "Keep up the fighting spirit," says a father to his son.

In *The Managerial Woman,* Hennig and Jardim note that girls have tended to excel only in one-to-one sports like ice skating, tennis, or golf—and even in those, girls quickly learned that winning might actually mean losing if they're playing against a man. Teenagers start losing even when they can win because a date for the prom is more important than a six-love tennis set. Betty Friedan has noted that teenaged girls tend to drop their special interests in favor of those that will appeal to men. "Men compete for awards," she says. "And we compete for men."

This kind of competition tends to continue throughout a

woman's life. The supervisor of an assembly line says that a woman on one shift will strive to beat the record of the woman who had the machine during an earlier shift—if they think it will bring them to his attention. "They only seem to be interested in a one-to-one competition for my approval," he comments. On the other hand, the men on the assembly line care about the department, and work for a *department* record.

Why? Because men learn a different kind of competition through team sports. Those working women who *have* had an opportunity to participate in team sports agree that athletics trained them for business in a way that their homes couldn't. Lynn is a middle manager in line for an upper management position. As a teenager, she thrived on competition and excelled in both sports and academics. "I never considered not beating a guy in sports or in class, although most of my girlfriends told me I'd never find a man that way. They preferred getting dates to hitting home runs. I wanted the home run—and the kind of man who wouldn't be threatened by it." Lynn says that team sports taught her when to push and when to let up, and how to get along with a *group* of people. When you're part of a team you can be the star or you can share the star's achievement. In either case, you have a common goal.

In *The Femininity Game,* Thomas Boslooper and Marcia Hayes quote social scientists John Roberts and Brian Sutton-Smith, who have made careful studies of the way games influence other aspects of a person's life. They discovered that business executives, politicians, and men in positions of power favored games that combined achievement and skill, while men in professional positions preferred games of strategy, like poker. Men in blue collar jobs were more interested in physical games. As a whole, women preferred games of strategy and chance. In other words, while men are in training for business success and power on the football field or at the poker table, women hone their feminine skills by playing bridge.

Men are far less apt to count on "luck" in getting ahead than women are. According to Caroline Bird, author of *Born Female*, several women who made it to the top before the days of women's lib and affirmative action credit personal competence, personality, connections, good luck, and the "breaks" for their success. Among these women she names Katherine Graham, publisher of *The Washington Post*; Philadelphia Judge Juanita Kidd Stout; advertising executive Mary Wells; and Anna Rosenberg Hoffman, who was a labor negotiator and Under Secretary of Defense in the administration of Franklin Delano Roosevelt. According to Bird, Hoffman had a sure instinct for the role appropriate to any situation, acting with some men like a sympathetic mother, with others as a bright gamin, a brusque executive, or even one of the boys. She also quotes Hoffman's advice, "A smart woman can take advantage of the fact that men do not see her as a threat."

As they have in the past, brilliant women or women with connections will find their way to the top of the heap, but the 1980s will begin the era when a woman doesn't have to be exceptional to make it. By learning business rules and becoming competitive the *average* woman can have the same opportunities as the *average* man.

------- • -------

Being competitive may mean having the courage to try a nontraditional job. You'll immediately be in competition with men because you'll be holding a position that used to go automatically to one of them. And at first they may not like having you around. A woman train conductor passes along this advice: "There's only one answer when a man says 'What are you doing in a man's job?' Say you like the work. You're not going to be such a threat if you're doing what you like. I also gave the men time to get used to me before I joined them in the off-duty room for cards. Now they respect me and I respect them—

although not all of them enjoy seeing a woman in an conductor's uniform."

A female carpenter whose partner told her, "I have my place
and you have yours, and yours isn't up on this roof," won his
grudging respect by never asking for special privileges. "Too
many times women don't compete fairly with men," she says.
"They expect to be given softer jobs that used to be reserved for
elderly men or men recovering from illness. We have to learn to
compete *equally.*"

Some men may cope with a new woman on the job by killing
her with kindness. An electrician recalls that the men were
always trying to teach her to use tools or read blueprints. They
were sure she was incompetent. "It wasn't until I finished my
work ahead of them that they realized I knew what I was doing.
After that, they treated me like one of the guys—so much so
that one day when I changed into a skirt after work I heard a
man saying, 'My God, Betty's got legs. You know, I'd forgotten
she wasn't a guy!' "

When you're working on a crew, you'll win your place by
demonstrating your competence and skill. It may be harder at
the office, where skills aren't so easy to spot and shortcomings
can be camouflaged. "We're living in an era when women are
pushed ahead too quickly," says one male executive. "They're
often put in positions without the necessary apprenticeship in
the company. They don't seem to know the business rules or
the way to get things done." This man uses the analogy of football to make his point. In football, for example, the clock can
run out while one team keeps the ball away from the opposi-
tion. The first team might not win by keeping the ball, but they
don't lose by any more than is necessary. In business, you can
let the clock run out on a poor idea by appointing a committee
to study it and write a report on it. In the office game, an inex-
perienced woman is often left carrying the ball in the backfield

while a man would have grounded the pass and gone back to the huddle to try a new play.

Socialized to lose gracefully, many women adopt a losing attitude at work. Men, on the other hand, know that when your team loses you rehash the game, learn from your mistakes, and then concentrate on your past wins and the ones you're going to have in the future. Women tend to give up and back off, assuming that rejection of an idea is a reflection of their general incompetence. Women don't ask the necessary questions that allow them to learn from a mistake. Moreover, women tend to see a failure as the *end* of a plan, while a man often sees that one failure may be a springboard to a new idea.

A corporate vice president explains that if one of his ideas is accepted he takes full credit for it, but if it doesn't work out he quickly moves away from it, shifting the responsibility to somebody lower in the department. Women, unfamiliar with this kind of deception, tend to either assume more responsibility for failure or stick with a poor idea longer. They simply don't know how to backtrack or move laterally.

———————

Recognizing and respecting your competition is as important as learning to compete. You don't want to adopt competitive behavior in inappropriate places. Competing with another member of a small office group may win you a point, but you may also lose an office ally who might be helpful later.

At times, winning can mean losing. If management planners introduce a new assembly-line technique over the strong protests of the workers, those workers may not give the new system a fair trial. In the long run, the "winning" planners might turn out to be the real losers.

Whenever possible, competitive businessmen avoid situations that involve making a clear choice between two diametrically opposed positions. Every businessman must learn how to say no without his client *knowing* that he said no. Then if later on he has to say yes he won't need to explain why he reversed himself.

You'll avoid getting trapped in win-lose situations at work if you begin to recognize the symptoms. If you're in a meeting and begin to feel under attack, or if you're pushing too hard to line up support from other committee members, you're headed for a win-lose situation. Catch yourself before it's too late and try to see the other person's reasoning. It may not work, but dignify it—and him—by your attention and thought. Avoid such flat statements as "The only way to do it is..." that leave little room for modification. Then if you do win, the fact that you've seriously considered the other person's ideas will still make him feel part of your team—and a winner too.

"I believe that a woman's insecurity about her *right* to be competing with men, coupled with her lack of familiarity with the office milieu, makes her want to 'be a good girl' and not bend the rules," says one male executive. "Men, on the other hand, know that bending the rules can often get you ahead." He tells of a corporate executive who was arranging to do business with an African subsidiary. He devised a complicated and clever method of shipping his product to meet a deadline, but he skipped paying several tariffs and the company was forced to pay a large fine. A woman would have been upset and ashamed at causing her corporation to lose so much money, but not this man. Instead, he concentrated on how close he had come to actually pulling off such a complicated deal. "The office admired his ingenious scheme, even though it hadn't been completely successful. Right and wrong never entered the picture. A woman would have been so hung up on legalities that she probably would never have contemplated such a maneuver in the first place. But Jack has gotten where he is, which is close to the top, by just this kind of approach."

The "legalities" that executive was talking about are the home-centered ethics many women bring with them to the office. But they can make you a loser at work if you choose the wrong kind of business. Every business has a different set of rules. You should be able to have a sure enough view of your own value system to see the difference between a corrupt system and a system that's merely different from yours. If you have too many doubts, you might be better off in a different field.

———————

Competitive behavior is not the only business plus learned from sports. Sports teach men that having the necessary number of teammates is more important than liking every one of them. They don't need to *like* teammates or coworkers. Women, however, insist on liking a person to work with or for them. "As long as a person is good at his job, I can work with him," says a male market researcher. But a woman is more apt to insist that a coworker be both good *and* likeable. You'll sabotage yourself by taking that approach.

An executive who has worked for three years for a boss he doesn't like sums it up this way: "I don't look for my friends at the office, and knowing that my boss isn't fond of me has challenged my competitive nature. I'm going to perform better just to show him up. In fact, I'm going after his job." He's obviously enjoying every bit of the fight. In a similar situation, a woman would probably be in flight. Not liking the boss (or not being liked by the boss) is reason enough to quit, request a transfer, or work so poorly that she's fired. "It's as bad as being stuck at a dance with a boy who doesn't like you. I can't work in conditions where I feel disliked," says an emotional woman whose attitude is limiting her growth. If *you* feel this way, you're overlooking the most important business rule—you're being paid to do a job, not to have a friend.

Competition and Teamwork

Your company has to make money, and everyone from a shipping clerk to the president is part of that goal. Men know this and have spent their lifetime developing styles of behavior that will help get them what they want. They maintain a network of associations with a variety of people—not necessarily all people they like, but all people who may be of help to them. They do favors and expect to be asked for favors in return. It's the business game, and it really isn't that different from sandlot baseball. A boy may throw down his bat, yell about an unfair call, and quit the game—but the next day he'll be back because he wants to play and he knows that the team needs a ninth player.

This same behavior continues in meeting rooms all across the country. Men use each other to get the job done, the order shipped, the price negotiated, the contract completed. Women are appalled by some of what goes on in the process because they tend to think of the office in terms of relationships and friendships.

Men on the job can often relate to each other in a way that women find impossible. Unlike the boy who comes back to play ball the next day, the little girl who leaves a game will often sulk or brood—and then she'll retaliate by telling nasty stories about the other players, or she'll tell her mother. There's a good chance that you'll want to do the same thing at work.

One woman remembers her reaction when her husband mentioned a disagreement he'd had with his boss. "Immediately I thought of every nasty bit of gossip I'd heard about him—but my husband didn't seem to be very interested in hearing it. He just accepted the fact that he disliked this man—the same way he accepted the fact that he'd have to work with him." His wife couldn't understand his approach because she'd been socialized to like people and to be liked in return. She can't simply accept those negative, uncomfortable feelings that come when she dislikes a person, so she tries to justify them.

Women are more apt to think this way because most of us were brought up to believe that nice girls didn't yell, scream, fight, punch, or say, "I hate you." When you were feeling furious your mother may have told you to turn the other cheek or look for the good in a person. Since it wasn't acceptable to work the feeling out directly, you learned to work it out indirectly by gathering ammunition against the other person.

The headmaster of a coeducational school explains the difference between his students in this way: "When the boys break a rule and get into trouble they may grouse a bit, but they accept their punishment and then it's over and done with. When a girl gets into trouble, the results are incredible. She cries, says the punishment is unfair, and often gets her revenge by stirring up all the girls in her dormitory. It becomes a vendetta." Later on this same girl will be mounting a vendetta against a boss or a coworker.

Although women are quite familiar with this kind of pettiness, they are often unaware of the male meaning of retaliation and revenge. "My masculine ego requires that nobody puts me down or gets the better of me. My identity is my business and I can't afford to lose," says one executive. A man may wait a long time for his revenge, says one businesswoman, but eventually he gets it. She tells of a coworker who was hired against the wishes of one man in the department. Six years later, when that man was the new head of the department, his first public act was to eliminate the job held for many years by his adversary. A woman might have forgotten her revenge by then.

One of the most personally destructive moves is "running to mother" by going over your boss's head. As a child, you probably ran to mother when somebody picked on you, and usually mother meted out some form of justice. Your department head is not your mother, and you'll strike out at work if you try to bypass your immediate superior. The chain of command at the office is like the one used by the military. Each person knows who they should report to. If you choose to go over your boss's head to complain, you'll often just be referred back to your boss—and the result will be a strained working atmosphere. You might even be fired, or be put in a position where you'll be incapable of making trouble.

Mary was a bright, energetic, and aggressive young editor who didn't get along with the head of her department. Instead of developing an effective way of working with him, she chose to establish a closer working relationship with Bill, the president of the company, who was involved in many of her department's projects. The arrangement seemed to work for Mary, but it created a lot of friction for her immediate boss— until the company was sold to a conglomerate, which decided to oust Bill. Mary was still responsible to the department head, but without her friend in court. After several months, she resigned.

If you try to bypass your boss, it obviously reflects on him and his improper management of his subordinates. One of the cardinal rules at the office is to make your boss look good. It's a two-way street. You make him look good, and he'll help you by recognizing your contribution and bringing it to the attention of others. If you don't discuss a problem with him first, he's going to feel betrayed—and he's certainly not going to consider you an effective member of his team!

Alice, a newspaper reporter, had difficulty getting the feature editor to approve some of her stories. She believed that her boss didn't have any good reason for rejecting her work, so the next time a story was turned down, Alice angrily declared that she was going to ask the managing editor for a second opinion. Aware that her boss was having some difficulty at the paper, Alice was sure that the managing editor would give her the green light. She walked into his office full of confidence, and she walked out without a job. The feature editor had gotten there first. Alice was told that she would have to find a way to work with the editor, which would be hard since she now refused to run any more of Alice's stories on her page. Alice had forced a confrontation, and it hadn't worked out. Keeping her head might have produced better results, and even if it didn't, a mannerly, businesslike resignation would have resulted in a good reference, and having her former boss as a resource. Men know how important it is to keep these kinds of channels open. Women tend to get emotional and slam shut the very doors they may need in the future.

It may take time to learn the kind of behavior patterns that will help you compete as part of a team. You'll find it easier if you remember these rules:

Competition isn't a sin, it's not unhealthy or unfeminine. Learning to compete will not make you "masculine." You can compete with good manners and still keep your femininity intact. Unfortunately, many new businesswomen try to compete by being harder and more aggressive than the men they work with. "Nothing puts me off more than one of those 'mock men' in grey flannel suits who try to throw their weight around," says a personnel director. "It's too bad they've chosen this approach. A woman can often accomplish a lot more by using charm than she can by being *over*aggressive."

Many women must also learn to compete without flaunting their authority. Didactic authority will mobilize all the hidden resentment men feel for women. After all, it was a woman who disciplined them when they were boys. You don't want to awaken those old, dormant resentments—you've got more than enough new ones to cope with.

The dean of an engineering school reported that the twenty women in this year's graduating class of seventy had all been snapped up by major corporations by March, while some of the men, who were equally qualified, still didn't have jobs in June.

Competition and Teamwork

The women are starting at salaries around twenty thousand dollars a year, while the men's are several thousand dollars lower.

Those women can expect resentment not only from their fellow classmates but also from the men at the offices where they'll be working. An executive explains it this way: "I found myself talking with a new female manager at a company training session. I hadn't any strong feelings about her one way or the other until she told me she was making only $5,000 less than I was. Immediately I felt hostile and resentful. After that, I was just watching for her mistakes. It's a shock after a lot of hard work in a company to have a woman brought in, knowing very little, and be given a paycheck that's almost equal to yours." You'll handle that kind of situation better by being quietly competitive instead of aggressively obnoxious.

Being vindictive and petty doesn't work. You'll be noticed in a negative way and labeled the office troublemaker if you try to get back at your coworkers or your boss. Even if it's only in a superficial fashion, try to get along with all the people you work with so that all the doors will be wide open for the future. Your contacts can be a crucial part of your progress, and you can't afford to alienate any of them—especially because you don't have as many as a man does in the first place!

You don't need to like the people you work with. Success on the job is not measured like a popularity contest. Learn to assess your working situation in a detached fashion and remember that this isn't the place for intense relationships. Determine what you want out of your working situation and whether you can get it. You may need to keep a psychological distance from an abrasive boss or coworker who's essential to your progress. Use the techniques outlined in the chapters on criticism, decision-making, and power to keep the relationship processed through your *head*, not your emotions. Study your personal power and criticism techniques until they become spontaneous. Remember that you're part of a team that works together to achieve a common goal. If you sense resentment, accept it. If you do your job well, your coworkers will eventually have to change their minds.

Sometimes healthy competition requires that you say "thank you, but no thank you." It means taking care of yourself *first.* You won't get ahead if you look for somebody *else* to do your job. It's okay for a man to open the door for you or even pull out your chair, but don't let him claim your work as his. Taking care of yourself means not being naive about the business process.

Competition can also mean disagreeing with the male point of view. Agree to disagree. Competition doesn't mean that you have to be harder or more masculine. In fact, you'll be far more effective if you compete in a feminine way, using your intuition and your good manners to form a package many men can't imitate.

How To Survive Success

———————⸱◂▸⸱———————

Cynthia Westover Alden held a wide variety of jobs. Her working career included rounding up cattle, teaching school, superintending both a tent factory and a candy factory, hunting for smugglers on the New York docks, supervising city street cleaning, acting as a customs inspector, and finally writing and editing. Her formula for success appeared in a magazine of the same name, and it's as applicable today as it was when it was first printed in 1900: "It is not so important what you do, but that you do it well. . . . Nobody who is ashamed of her present industry deserves to get advanced to anything else. . . . That same fatal lack of earnestness would pursue you, and you would discover too late that every occupation has its drawbacks. . . . A woman will be treated by male employers with dignity and fairness if she cultivates . . . conscience and poise. She has no right to exact more deference than other employees because she is a woman. . . . There is no reason you should not succeed . . . outside of yourself."

———————⸱◂▸⸱———————

Jennifer is an update of Cynthia Alden's successful woman. Her energy, honesty, and openness about herself are as refreshing as they are contagious. It's easy to see why she's rated the most popular professor by the students at the West Coast university where she teaches social psychology. Undeniably, forty-year-old Jennifer wears the label of success. She has tripled her salary in the past six years, published three books and hundreds of articles, and received more awards and grants than any other professor at the university.

Jennifer has mastered the conflicts between her training as a woman and the realities of the working world. She didn't complete her education until ten years and three children after leaving college. And when she chose a teaching career, she found that many of the values she brought from the home didn't fit in the academic community, which often slams the door in the face of a woman who wants more than an associate professorship. But Jennifer became a winner, and the strategies she learned can help you gain not only success, but also the ability to *handle* that success.

I was an only child with a brilliant and strong father—a chemist—who was forty-five when I was born. He taught me that it didn't matter if I could type or spell—in fact, if I could that would probably be all that was expected of me. Instead, I learned to stretch my mind by looking at concepts. I was learning leadership when I was four years old, an age when most little girls are having tea parties with their dolls. My father created an explorer's club for the family, and rotated the offices of president, vice president, and chief cook and bottle washer. Every third week I was in charge of planning an expedition for the three of us.

My father's views of success were pretty straightforward, but my mother's were somewhat conflicting. She believed that a woman's goal was to marry a good man and belong to the Colonial Dames—but even within the limitations of this world she achieved a lot because she was a smart woman who successfully channeled her achievement drive. She was very active in chari-

ty and volunteer work, and she was very good at it. These days, many women channel their achievement drive into a career, and then they're disappointed because their personal lives, their marriage prospects, aren't always enhanced by their work. A man's social eligibility increases with a good job and a salary, but women often have to trade social and sexual relationships for their monetary rewards. In fact, many women choose not to pursue a better job or an advanced degree for fear of threatening the man in their lives. My mother solved the conflict between her drives and her personal needs by being a super wife, mother, and volunteer. Other women do it by going into less threatening nurturing professions like nursing and teaching. Young women today are better able to minimize this kind of conflict, but it's still a force to be reckoned with.

It was certainly a much tougher issue back in the fifties when I was in college. In my junior year, my father died, and I plummeted from being an exceptional student to being a mediocre one. Looking back, I know that I really missed my father's support, particularly because my interest in a career wasn't the traditional one for a woman. Without my father to guide me, I turned to my mother and chose her route. I dropped out of school, married, and had three children. It took ten years to motivate myself to go back to school and rediscover the career I'd left behind. While I stayed home, I enjoyed my kids but I loathed the confinement and lack of intellectual stimulation. I felt as if I were stagnating. My return to school stimulated the whole family—being in college with my children's generation has made me more aware of their conflicts and lifestyle. And at times it made me question my own.

After I got my PhD, I applied for a teaching position at a local college and began to learn about the realities of the academic world. I didn't always like what I saw, and at times I felt that I had to choose between my personal satisfaction and my professional advancement. For me, personal success in-

175

volves meeting and setting my own individual goals and living by my own standards of right and wrong. Like many women, I often saw only one clear-cut choice when I considered the conflicts between personal and professional success. The trick is to learn different ways of seeing a problem so that the two can work together instead of against each other.

A good example of this was the whole process I went through to be granted tenure. When I first became eligible I was told that I wouldn't receive tenure because we were in the middle of a budget crunch. No one mentioned the other reason—I was a woman in a male-dominated department. I had spent more time teaching than my associates did because I refused to turn my lectures over to a graduate student so I could use the time to write. In my opinion, the man who did receive tenure had sold out. He kept notoriously short office hours, rarely taught, and had minimal requirements for his students because he didn't want to be bothered grading papers. I believed in my students and made the choice I thought was right. But I might still have received my tenure if I'd been a smart businesswoman. I wasn't then, but I am now.

Academia, like business, protects itself against women by being vague about the standards used for who gets what. When I started at the university I was told the requirements for tenure—teaching, publishing, and receiving grants—but I never got anything in writing. It simply never occurred to me that men would lie. In order to succeed in a world that's dominated by male ethics, I had to learn about male duplicity. My case for tenure included an excellent rating from my students and as many awards and published articles as the man who received tenure, yet for me the rules shifted and the committee trivialized everything I had done. Like many women, I didn't realize that there's an elasticity in standards. And I didn't know how to document my case.

By the second time around, I'd learned to sell myself like a product, and I'd forgotten the traditional female modesty. I assessed my strengths, and whenever a person mentioned a weakness I was able to counterbalance it with a strength. I also figured the total monetary value of those strengths. For example, another professor and I taught ninety percent of the social science students in our department, so I added up the amount of money that I personally brought the college and the department in tuition rebate. It was quite a sum, because all my classes were filled to capacity. I rewrote my resumé like a publicity release, telling what I personally had contributed and how many grants and awards I had won for the university. Yes, I was boasting, something I'd been brought up to believe a nice girl didn't do. But that kind of blowing your own horn is what gets you noticed.

Today I've learned to document everything that I'm told and to send copies to key people. I don't believe that women need to duplicate male ethics, but we do need to protect ourselves. This can be a difficult hurdle to cross because we're used to seeing men as people who'll look after and protect us, not rip us off.

Take the question of equality in wages. Most women have been brought up to believe that it's bad to talk about money. They stay cute, sweet, and helpless; they appreciate whatever they get—and of course they don't get what they're worth. You've got to get our there and fight for yourself. Last year my salary worked out to be $4,000 less than it should have been. Instead of arguing, I sent the faculty committee a list of my activities for the past month, including teaching, TV appearances, radio spots, banquets, awards, publicity trips, and editorial conferences for the book I've just finished. The list proved my value to the university and backed up my statement that another school might be eager to have me—at the salary I wanted. I sent out twenty copies of the letter. They coughed up the $4,000.

Too often, women get into the habit of underestimating

themselves. A woman needs to learn how to substantiate her case when she's after a better position or more money. You'll get ahead if you deliver the goods and insist on due credit for the delivery. It isn't a fair world yet for women, but we can make it a lot fairer by getting rid of our out-of-date cultural luggage and learning from each other. We also need to take more chances. I've had to learn a lot of things by making mistakes.

I've also had to realize that success has its price, particularly when it comes to loneliness and lack of personal privacy. After all, the higher you go, the fewer people there will be at your level—and the more people there will be to make demands of you. In many cases, success has meant giving up some of the things I want to do. I get tired of public appearances, I miss browsing in libraries or reading a book because I want to not because I need to professionally. I miss not spending more time with my husband and children—although this is something of a fantasy since my husband is a doctor who works just as hard as I do, and the kids are now teenagers who don't want or need a mother hanging over their shoulders. When I think about it, I realize that my children have matured and become self-sufficient because I work. My job is my network to a life filled with warm, supportive people. It's a rich life, and it's a good place to be.

Jennifer's success strategies can be used by *every* woman. You can begin building *yours* today by following these ground rules:

Acquire a realistic attitude about yourself and your job. Remember Murphy's law—nothing is as easy as it looks; everything takes longer than you expect; and if anything can go wrong, it will, at the worst possible moment. Things go wrong at work, just the way they do at home. Once you can accept this, you can stop brooding about mistakes or injustices and *learn* from them. Don't give up because you didn't win the first time—the second time around you may have learned enough to win even bigger!

Deliver the goods. Whether or not you're able to produce will be the bottom line when it comes to success, so be sure that you continue to grow *with* your job. Taking some time to learn your job is fine, and only to be expected, but once you've learned, stop being a modest pupil and become an assertive employee. Have ideas, look for *better* ways to do a job, and take a chance on those better ways. Give yourself the opportunity to step into the limelight by taking pride in your achievements.

Know your office reality. The office is *not* one big happy family. There are going to be as many internal battles at the office as there are external ones. The only way you can get ahead is to know how everything operates, understand the guidelines and the standard procedures, and understand the *people* who are working with them.

Set a series of goals and meet them. Look at what you want to do and then figure out how you're going to get there. Plot your course in manageable steps and build on your past successes. Keep setting new goals once you've met the old ones. Life is a dynamic process, and your priorities may change, but your personal growth will continue if you never stop challenging yourself.

Know the price of your goal. Everything has a price, but it's up to you to make a decision on whether you choose to pay that price. According to studies made by social scientist Matina Horner, a man's social life and supply of marriage partners keep pace with his success—but for a woman the opposite is true. Success can bring loneliness. You may have to give up some close office friendships or sacrifice your social life because of the demands of your job. You may find that the rewards of your job aren't worth the strains on your personal life.

Work to achieve a balanced life. Allow time for yourself. Women need to learn unwinding strategies just as much as they need to learn winning strategies. You need to turn off the wheels to regenerate and rejuvenate. You'll think better and be more productive if you can take time to free your mind from the office. You can soothe your tensions and achieve perspective on your working life by giving yourself time to *relax*.

———————•—•———————

Now you're ready to use all these strategies to chart your *own* success story. You can develop your own style, one that announces to the world that you have all the resources within yourself to have what you want and be what you want. You've made your own choices and taken your own risks. You know what meeting your goals will mean, and you're willing to take responsibility for achieving them. You don't need to start with connections or money. You only need two things, a belief in yourself and a willingness to learn the techniques and attitudes that will make sure *you're* winning at work.

Selected Bibliography

―――――――

General Interest

Born Female, by Caroline Bird. New York: Pocket Books, 1969. $1.50, 240 pp.   A highly sensitive book that describes what it's like to be born a female in American society. The chapter on "Loophole Women" is especially recommended.

Enterprising Women, by Caroline Bird. New York: New American Library, 1976. $1.95, 256 pp.   An inspiring book on the accomplishments of women throughout U.S. history.

The Feminine Mystique, by Betty Friedan. New York: Dell, 1963. $1.95, 410 pp.   This is the trailblazer of the women's movement, the book that exploded the myth of the happy housewife. It should be a reference for your library.

CHAPTER 1.   Goodbye Guilt

Guilt-Free Existence, by Paula and Dick McDonald. New York: Ballantine, 1977. $2.25, 363 pp.   A somewhat wordy book in which the authors make a good case for the correlation between your moral values and the time you were born. The first few chapters are the best.

Man's World, Woman's Place, by Elizabeth Janeway. New

York: Dell, 1971. $2.95, 317 pp. Janeway explores the social and psychological forces that have influenced the position of women throughout history. Of particular interest are her positive data on the children of working mothers. A good antidote to the guilt you may feel over going to work.

When I Say No, I Feel Guilty, by Manuel J. Smith. New York: Bantam, 1975. $2.25, 321 pp. A good book on systematic assertive therapy. Provides dialogue to help you practice becoming assertive.

CHAPTER 2. Ride Out Rejection

My Mother, Myself, by Nancy Friday. New York: Dell, 1979. $2.50, 425 pp. This book explores the author's relationship with her mother. Interesting reading, and good psychological insights that may be helpful if you're trying to understand the roots of your behavior patterns.

Sisters, by Elizabeth Fishel. New York: Morrow, 1979. $9.95, 345 pp. The chapters called "The Family Constellation" and "Inside the Family Crucible and Beyond" are recommended for readers who want to explore their early sibling relationships and birth position in terms of their future achievements. Also touches on mother-daughter and father-daughter relationships.

What Color is Your Parachute? A Practical Manual for Job Hunters and Career-Changers, by Richard Nelson Bolles. Berkeley, California: Ten Speed Press, 1978. $5.95, 290 pp. An excellent book that provides both good reviews of standard job-hunting techniques and pointers for unique strategies. Also includes a good list of resources. Informative, witty and creative. You should have it as a reference book.

CHAPTER 3. I Don't Know Why He Hired Me

Kicking the Fear Habit, by Manuel J. Smith. New York: Bantam, 1978. $2.45, 307 pp. An informative book on fears that provides behavioral techniques for overcoming particular phobias such as fear of heights or fear of flying.

Nothing to Fear: Coping with Phobias, by Kent Fraser. New York: Doubleday, 1977. $7.95, 204 pp. An informative and helpful general study.

Overcoming Worry and Fear, by Paul Hauck. Philadelphia: Westminster, 1975. $3.50, 112 pp. A short and interesting book based on the views of rational emotion therapy—that fear and worry are irrational beliefs that must be challenged.

Stop Running Scared, by Herbert Fensterheim and Jean Baer. New York: Rawson, 1977. $10.95, 326 pp. A popular book on overcoming fears and phobias. Provides several good behavior modification techniques, illustrated by case histories.

What Are You Afraid Of? by John Wood. Englewood Cliffs, New Jersey: Prentice-Hall, 1976. $2.95, 178 pp. Cites literary sources in discussing aspects of fear. The chapter on fear's relationship to other emotions is particularly interesting.

Your Erroneous Zones, by Dr. Wayne Dyer. New York: Avon, 1977. $2.25, 253 pp. Dr. Dyer's conversational style really hits home. We liked the chapter on "The Useless Emotions—Guilt and Worry," particularly Dyer's discussion of the psychological payoffs for choosing worry.

CHAPTER 4. **Decisions, Risks, and Mistakes**

How to Decide: A Workbook for Women, by Nellie T. Schotz, Judith S. Prince, and Gordon P. Miller. New York: Avon, 1975. $4.95, 124 pp. An effective means of strengthening decision-making capabilities for readers who enjoy using workbooks. A minimal amount of text.

The Managerial Woman, by Margaret Hennig and Anne Jardim. New York: Pocket Books, 1979. $2.50, 255 pp. Although the style is somewhat scholarly, this is an excellent sourcebook for women in management. The middle section, which was originally part of Hennig's doctoral thesis, explores the lives of twenty-five women executives who made it to the top.

The New Assertive Woman, by Lynn Z. Bloom, Karen Coburn, and Joan Pearlman. New York: Delacorte, 1975. $7.95, 230 pp. A basic book on assertiveness training for women. Easy reading; a good starting point for beginners.

CHAPTER 5. The Criticism Crumble

The Assertive Woman, by Stanlee Phelps and Nancy Austin. San Luis Obispo, California: Impact, 1975. $3.95, 177 pp. An early book on assertiveness training for women that includes interesting chapters on compliments, criticism, and rejection.

Self Creation, by Dr. George Weinberg. New York: Avon, 1979. $2.50, 220 pp. A valuable self-help book that covers all the psychological basics, offering practical solutions and easy practice steps. Of particular interest are the chapters on criticism, making complaints, and making up your mind.

CHAPTER 6. Crisis Thinking

Relax: How You Can Feel Better, Reduce Stress, and Overcome Tension, edited by John White and James Fadiman. New York: Dell, 1976. $1.95, 253 pp. A fine collection of relaxation techniques that gives the reader a choice of several helpful methods.

CHAPTER 7. Anger is Good For You

Anger: How to Recognize and Cope with It, by Leo Madow. New York: Scribner's, 1972. $2.45, 132 pp. Psychoanalytically oriented. Especially recommended is the chapter on the relationship between suppressed anger and physical and psychological problems.

The Angry Book, by Dr. Theodore Isaac Rubin. New York: Macmillan, 1969. $1.25, 223 pp.   A popular book that includes a lengthy discussion of how people sabotage themselves when they suppress anger. Also provides ways to recognize how you handle your own anger. Easy reading.

The Book of Hope: How Women Can Overcome Depression, by Helen A. De Rosis, M.D., and Victoria Pellegrino. New York: Bantam, 1977. $2.25, 336 pp.   A self-help book that provides some basic, but interesting insights.

Creative Aggression, by Dr. George R. Bach and Dr. Herb Goldberg. New York: Avon, 1974. $1.95, 337 pp.   A provocative, popularly written book that claims "nice" people are really very angry. Provides good psychological insights on how the suppressed anger of adults could affect their children. If you only have time to read one book on anger, this is the one.

The Intimate Enemy, by George Bach and Peter Wyden. New York: Avon, 1968. $1.75, 384 pp.   Concentrates on constructive releases of anger. Especially oriented toward couples. Provides step-by-step techniques on how to release anger constructively and "fight fair." Highly informative.

CHAPTER 8.   Personal Power

Body Language, by Julius Fast. New York: Pocket Books, 1970. $1.75, 183 pp.   A popular book on the meaning of nonverbal communication. The author talks about personal space and body language in an easy-to-read and entertaining style.

How to Read a Person Like a Book, by Gerard I. Nierenberg and Henry H. Calero. New York: Cornerstone, 1972. $2.95,

184 pp. Concentrates on body language in business situations. Be careful, though, not to fall into the authors' trap of interpreting one gesture as having only one meaning.

Power! by Michael Korda. New York: Ballantine, 1975. $1.95, 311 pp. An excellent book in which the author explores such subjects as power areas, power games, power exercises, and power symbols. Entertaining and enjoyable reading that includes interesting tidbits on powerful people.

Pulling Your Own Strings, by Dr. Wayne Dyer. New York: Avon, 1979. $2.75, 262 pp. Read "Declaring Yourself a Non-Victim" and then check out the questions at the back of the book to see whether or not you really *are* a "non-victim."

The Silenced Majority, by Kirsten Amundsen. Englewood Cliffs, New Jersey: Prentice-Hall, 1971. $2.95, 184 pp. An informative book on women and political power.

The Territorial Imperative, by Robert Ardrey. New York: Dell, 1966. $1.50, 355 pp. A highly enlightening anthropology book that makes the premise that territoriality is genetically determined. You'll need time to digest Ardrey's ideas, but it's worth the effort.

The Woman's Dress for Success Book, by John T. Molloy. New York: Warner, 1977. $3.95, 187 pp. An excellent book on how to build an effective business wardrobe, all the way from styles and colors to makeup and accessories. Molloy also notes regional differences. A good reference book.

CHAPTER 9. Who's Boss in the Office Family?

The Gamesman: The New Corporate Leaders, by Michael Maccoby. New York: Bantam, 1978. $2.75, 285 pp. You can better understand your boss by fitting him into Maccoby's corporate mold as craftsman, gamesman, or company man. Insights into corporate life will also be helpful to new women executives.

Peoplemaking, by Virginia Satir. Palo Alto, California: Science and Behavior Books, 1972. $4.95, 304 pp. A highly entertaining book on human relationships. Satir's discussion of patterns of communication is particularly recommended.

Winning Through Intimidation, by Robert Ringer. New York: Fawcett, 1973. $2.25, 303 pp. We're not fans of Ringer's, but you'll find some new techniques here for business operations— and some old insights that remain valid. It's likely that you'll find people like those Ringer describes in *your* office family.

CHAPTER **10.** **Competition and Teamwork**

The Femininity Game, by Thomas Boslooper and Marcia Hayes. New York: Stein and Day, 1974, $1.95, 224 pp. The authors explore the socialization process of boys and girls in terms of winning, losing, and competition. Includes a lot of information on women in sports and historical references to female aggressive behavior.

Games Mother Never Taught You, by Betty Harragan. New York: Warner, 1977. $2.50, 399 pp. A very informative book that examines the relationship between the corporate world, sports, and the military. Very well written and documented. Highly recommended.

The Managerial Woman, by Margaret Hennig and Anne Jardim. New York: Pocket Books, 1979. $2.50, 255 pp. An excellent sourcebook for women in management, although the style is sometimes a bit scholarly. We particularly recommend the chapters on "Patterns of Difference and Their Implications" and "The Middle Management Career Path."

EPILOGUE: **How to Survive Success**

The Broken Heart, by James J. Lynch. New York: Basic Books, 1977. $10.95, 271 pp.   A highly informative but technical book that discusses the medical consequences of loneliness. Be sure to read this if you're having trouble deciding on a career— it will help you realize the necessity of integrating work, family, and companionship.

Success, by Michael Korda. New York: Random House, 1977. $8.95, 297 pp.   Not as good as Korda's *Power!,* although it does contain an interesting section on women and success. However, the book as a whole doesn't reveal anything really new.

The Two Paycheck Marriage, by Caroline Bird. New York: Rawson, Wade, 1979. $8.95, 294 pp.   A valuable look at how many couples handle the priorities and problems of managing two incomes.

Index

Index

About the Authors

ANNE LORIMER is a journalist who has spent the past five years covering women's issues. Her work has been published in numerous national magazines and newspapers, most notably *The Christian Science Monitor*.

DR. FLORENCE SEAMAN is a clinical psychologist who has pioneered in group therapy for women. Before concentrating on her private practice and her workshops for women, Dr. Seaman worked as a consultant for Project Headstart and developed programs for the National Institute of Mental Health. She has also coordinated several state and federal mental health programs.